P9-EGN-662

Egypt

Egypt

By Ann Heinrichs

Enchantment of the World™
Second Series

Children's Press®
An Imprint of Scholastic Inc.

New York Toronto London Auckland Sydney
Mexico City New Delhi Hong Kong
Danbury, Connecticut

Frontispiece: Shopkeeper in Khan al-Khalili bazaar in Cairo

Consultant: Laura E. Bier, PhD, Associate Professor of History, Georgia Institute of Technology

Please note: All statistics are as up-to-date as possible at the time of publication.

Book production by The Design Lab

Library of Congress Cataloging-in-Publication Data

Heinrichs, Ann.
Egypt/by Ann Heinrichs.—Rev. ed.
p. cm.—(Enchantment of the world. Second series.)
Includes bibliographical references and index.
ISBN-13: 978-0-531-25309-0 (lib. bdg.)
ISBN-10: 0-531-25309-0 (lib. bdg.)
1. Egypt—Juvenile literature. I. Title. II. Series.
DT49.H45 2012
962—dc23 2011031119

No part of this publication may be reproduced in whole or in part, or stored in a retrieval system, or transmitted in any form or by any means, electronic, mechanical, photocopying, recording, or otherwise, without written permission of the publisher. For information regarding permission, write to Scholastic Inc., 557 Broadway, New York, NY 10012.

© 2012 by Scholastic Inc.
All rights reserved. Published in 2012 by Children's Press, an imprint of Scholastic Inc.
Printed in the United States of America 113

SCHOLASTIC, CHILDREN'S PRESS, and associated logos are trademarks and/or registered trademarks of Scholastic Inc.
1 2 3 4 5 6 7 8 9 10 R 21 20 19 18 17 16 15 14 13 12

Acknowledgments

I am grateful to Martha and Magdy Farahat for their hospitality during my stay in Egypt and for their insights into Egyptian life and culture; to Egyptologist Manal Helmy for giving me a grand tour of all of Egyptian history and culture; and to Danny Brady and Wayne Redmond of Imaginative Traveller for making sure my visit was the ultimate in education, hardship, and fun.

Contents

Cover photo:
An Egyptian man and his camel

CHAPTER

ONE Children of the Revolution **8**

TWO Black Land, Red Land **14**

THREE Nature in the Desert **26**

FOUR From Pharaohs to Presidents **36**

FIVE Governing the Nation **62**

SIX Making a Living **74**

SEVEN Crowded Cities, Common Bonds **88**

EIGHT Spiritual Lives **98**

NINE Culture and Fun **108**

TEN Many Flavors of Life **116**

Coral reef

Timeline **128**

Fast Facts **130**

To Find Out More **134**

Index **136**

Steppe eagle

Children of the Revolution

THROWN ROCKS AND SHATTERED GLASS FLY THROUGH the air, and rubber bullets whiz by. Eleven-year-old Yousuf dons a hard hat for protection. Meanwhile, fourteen-year-old Salma worries about her father. He is a doctor who is caring for injured people. Other children carry signs, join in chants, and sing protest songs. Many have their faces painted with the colors of the Egyptian flag—red, white, and black.

Opposite: **In 2011, thousands of Egyptians took to the streets to demand a change in their government.**

These kids are taking part in a momentous event in their nation's history—the 2011 Egyptian revolution. They are among the thousands of young people who joined their families in Tahrir Square. This plaza in Cairo, Egypt, was the site of an eighteen-day demonstration.

Though violence sometimes flared up, it was a peaceful revolution. It started on January 25, 2011, when Egyptians began to gather in the square. They came to protest the thirty-year rule of President Hosni Mubarak. Protesters were fed up with government corruption, police brutality, and widespread poverty and unemployment. Freedom of speech was another issue. Under Mubarak, it was a crime to criticize the government. But Egyptians had reasons to be optimistic.

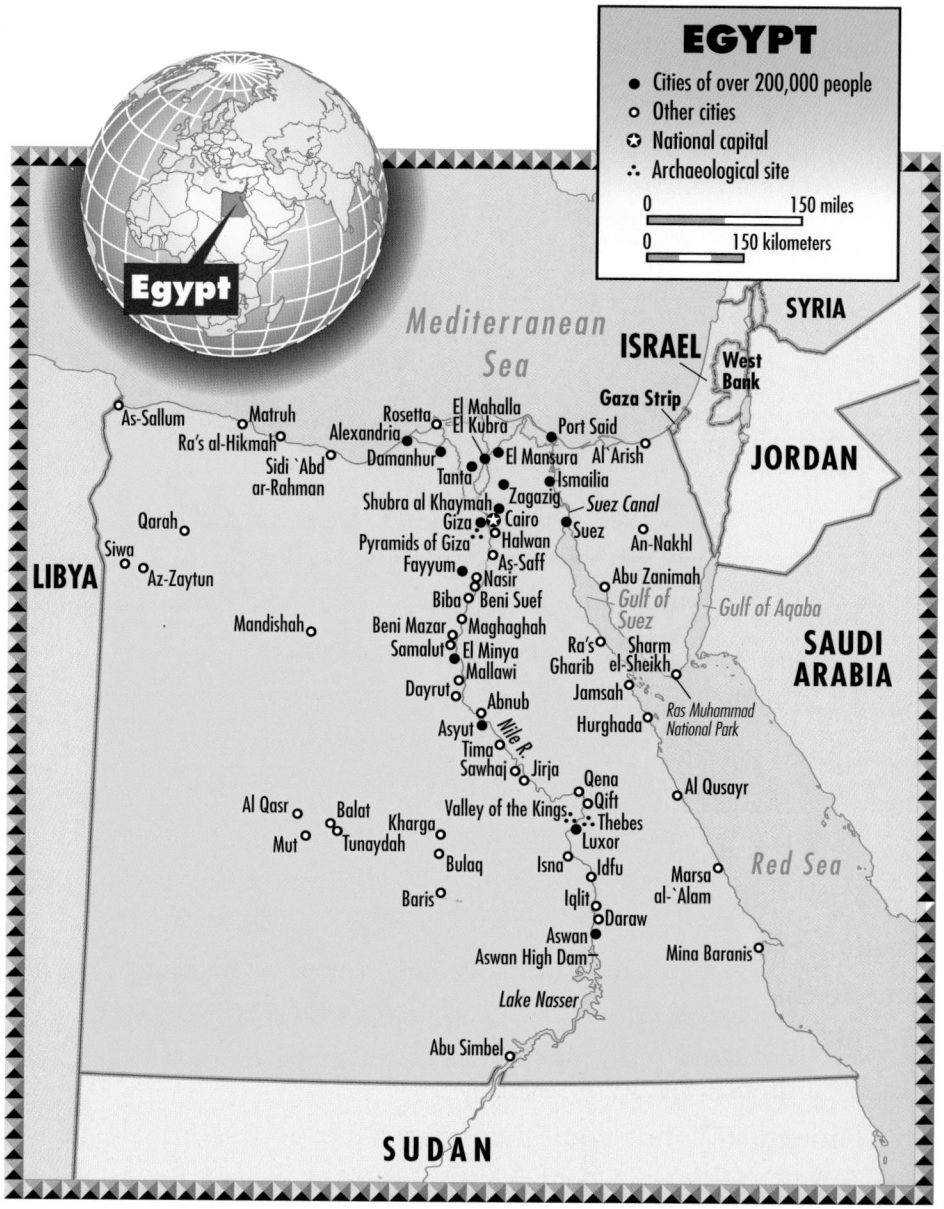

A wave of unrest was sweeping across the Arab world, from North Africa to the Arabian Peninsula. Citizens were rising up against harsh regimes. This movement was called the Arab Spring because it was a time of new beginnings. Egyptians rejoiced with their neighbors in Tunisia, another North

African country. Only eleven days earlier, demonstrators there had succeeded in ousting their president. Now Egyptians felt empowered to do the same.

Citizens of all ages and social classes came together in Tahrir Square. Differences in religious beliefs were unimportant. The overwhelming majority of Egyptians are Muslims, followers of the religion of Islam. Yet many members of the Christian minority were there as well. All were united by a common purpose and a sense of community. "There were many challenges, but all the protesters were like one big family," observed fourteen-year-old Aya.

Hosni Mubarak served as president for thirty years before the 2011 protests forced him from power.

Hundreds of thousands of Egyptians gathered in Tahrir Square in downtown Cairo to celebrate the end of Mubarak's rule.

By February 1, hundreds of thousands of people had assembled in the square. Many families had set up tents there. They were determined to stay until their demands were met. And they demanded nothing less than Mubarak's resignation. Parents brought their children so they could witness a great event in Egyptian history. "It's the birth of freedom, and I'm proud," said one parent. "Witnessing this event will engrave in them love for this nation—loyalty, freedom, and respecting change."

Finally, on the night of February 11, Mubarak announced he would resign. Wild cheers arose from the crowd. Lively music and joyful songs resounded throughout the square. "I was so happy and excited, I kept hugging people I don't know," said one teenager. According to another boy, "We felt that God has helped us finish this." The children of the revolution will remember this day forever. And they will proudly tell their own children and grandchildren how they helped change the face of Egypt.

The Egyptian revolution was a high point in a long and eventful history. Egypt is home to one of the oldest civilizations on earth. Ancient Egyptians built fabulous pyramids, temples, and tombs that still amaze us today. Almost twenty-five hundred years ago, the Greek historian Herodotus gazed upon these wonders. "Nowhere are there so many marvelous things," he wrote, "nor in the world besides are there to be seen so many things of unspeakable greatness." Invasions and conquests changed the face of Egypt down through the centuries. Yet today's Egyptians remain well-grounded in Arabic culture, which permeates their everyday lives. This shared culture unites them with millions of others throughout the Arab world.

Despite the 2011 revolution, Egypt still faces many difficulties. Poverty and unemployment continue to be serious problems. New leaders may cling to old ways, and new laws may not assure the hoped-for freedoms. But Egyptians look to the future with confidence. Inflamed with the spirit of the revolution, they know they can meet tomorrow's challenges.

Schoolchildren walk past piles of garbage in a poor neighborhood in Cairo.

Black Land, Red Land

EGYPT IS A DESERT WITH A RIVER RUNNING THROUGH it. Almost 97 percent of Egypt's land is desert. It has one major waterway, the life-giving Nile, which is the longest river in the world. The Nile flows north across the entire length of the country and empties into the Mediterranean Sea. It separates Egypt's Western and Eastern Deserts.

Opposite: **Crops grow well in fields near the Nile. Farther away from the river, farming flourishes only in desert oases and irrigated areas.**

Ancient Egyptians called their land Kemet, meaning "black land," for the rich soil of the Nile River valley. Deshret, the "red land," was the surrounding desert.

Egypt covers an area almost as large as the U.S. states of Texas and New Mexico combined. It is slightly larger than the Canadian province of British Columbia. Southern Egypt is known as Upper Egypt because the land there has a higher elevation. The southern part of the Nile River is called the Upper Nile. Lower Egypt and the Lower Nile are in northern Egypt, where the land is lower.

Nearly all of Egypt is in the continent of Africa. The Sinai Peninsula is the only part of Egypt that lies in Asia.

The Suez Canal connects the Mediterranean Sea and the Gulf of Suez. It allows ships to travel from Europe to Asia without having to go all the way around Africa.

The Sinai is in Egypt's northeast corner beyond the Gulf of Suez and the Suez Canal. This canal marks the dividing line between the two continents.

The Deserts

Egypt's two largest land regions are the Western Desert and the Eastern Desert. The Western Desert, also called the Libyan Desert, covers about two-thirds of the country. It is part of North Africa's great Sahara Desert, which extends west into Libya and south into Sudan.

The Western Desert is a vast expanse of rippling sand, blown about by the winds. Rocky ridges jut out here and there. In some places, the sand piles up to form graceful dunes.

The desert sands can be destructive, however, when they blow over farmlands and villages. The Qattara Depression, a sunken area in the north, is Egypt's lowest point at 435 feet (133 meters) below sea level.

The Eastern Desert is also called the Arabian Desert. That's because long ago, Egypt was joined to the Arabian Peninsula. From the east bank of the Nile, the Eastern Desert slopes gently upward into rocky hills that line the Red Sea coast. Deep ravines called wadis cut through the hills.

Few people live in the Eastern Desert, but several small towns lie along the coast. The northern coastal waters of Hurghada, a center for Egypt's Red Sea oil-drilling activities, are severely polluted. South of the town, though, the water is clean enough to attract divers who explore the coast's spectacular coral reefs.

Fish swarm around a colorful coral reef in the Red Sea.

Egypt's Geographic Features

Highest Elevation: Jabal Katrina (Mount Catherine), 8,668 feet (2,642 m) above sea level

Lowest Elevation: Qattara Depression, 435 feet (133 m) below sea level

Greatest Distance, North to South: 636 miles (1,024 km)

Greatest Distance, East to West: 770 miles (1,240 km)

Longest River: Nile, about 900 miles (1,450 km) long in Egypt; about 4,132 miles (6,650 km) in total length

Largest Lake: Lake Nasser, about 2,030 square miles (5,260 sq km)

Highest Recorded Temperature: 122.5°F (50.3°C) at Kharga on June 9, 1961

Lowest Recorded Temperature: 16.2°F (–8.8°C) at Nakhl on January 16, 2008

Driest City: Aswan, 0.02 inches (0.05 cm) average annual precipitation

Wettest City: Alexandria, 7.9 inches (20 cm) average annual precipitation

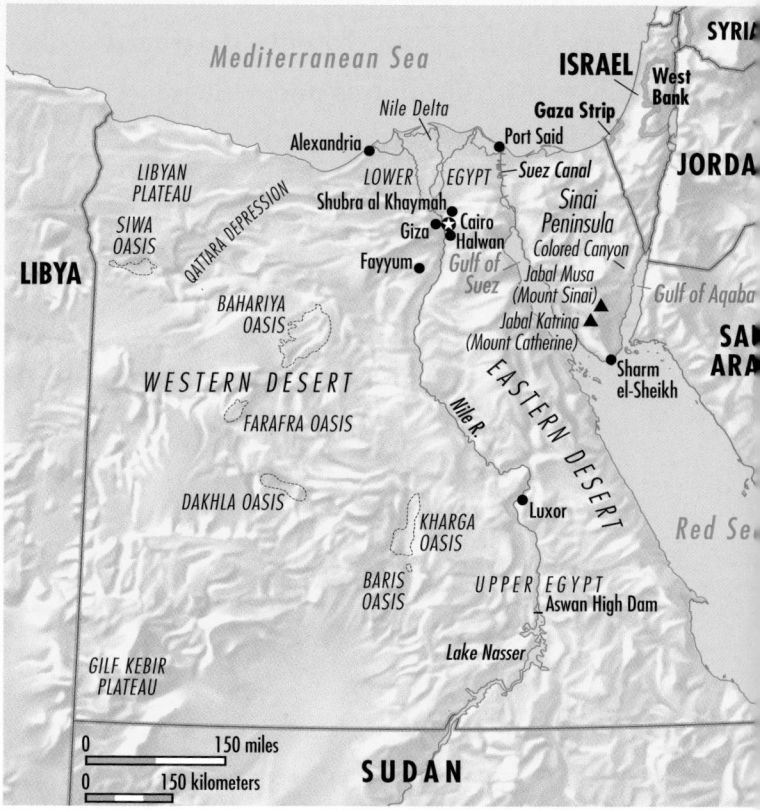

The Nile Valley and Delta

The Nile River has nourished Egypt's farms for thousands of years. Without the Nile, Egypt would be one huge desert. The waters of the Nile flow from two sources. Upstream in central Sudan, two rivers—the White Nile and the Blue Nile—join to form one river. The White Nile, the longer branch, rises in Burundi, deep in the heart of Africa. From there to the Mediterranean Sea, the Nile is about 4,132 miles (6,650 kilometers) long. Most of the Nile's water, however, comes from the Blue Nile. This branch rises in the highlands of Ethiopia. The torrential summer rains there cause annual floods in Egypt.

Near Cairo, Egypt's capital city, the Nile fans out into many streams that empty into the Mediterranean. When these streams flood, they deposit rich sediment on the land. This fertile area is called the delta, after the Greek letter shaped like a triangle (Δ). The delta stretches about 100 miles (160 km) from north to south and about 150 miles (240 km) along the coast. Almost all of Egypt's farmland is in the delta and in a narrow strip along the river. Most of Egypt's people live in these areas, too. Alexandria is a historic delta city that sits right on the seacoast.

Flooding from the Nile River has deposited nutrients on the nearby land, making it good for growing crops.

Palm trees flourish in Siwa Oasis.

Western Desert Oases

An oasis is an area in the desert where underground water flows to the surface. In Egypt's Western Desert oases, the water gushes up in springs and gathers into ponds and wells surrounded by tall date palms and lush gardens. In some oases, the underground waters feed rich, green valleys.

Oases closest to the Nile are called the New Valley oases and include Bahariya, Farafra, Dakhla, and Kharga. Long ago, a branch of the Nile flowed through them. Other oases are Baris, south of Kharga, and Siwa, near the Libyan border.

Looking at Egypt's Cities

Alexandria (below) was founded by Alexander the Great around 332 BCE. As a center of science and learning, it became one of the greatest cities of the ancient world. The Library of Alexandria was the most famous library of ancient times. Today, with a population of about 4,100,000, Alexandria is Egypt's second-largest city, trailing only the capital city of Cairo. Alexandria is also the country's major seaport, with a busy harbor on the Mediterranean Sea. Many sites recall the city's glorious past. The Greco-Roman Museum preserves objects from Alexandria's old period. The Bibliotheca Alexandrina, opened in 2002, was built in honor of Alexandria's ancient library. The city's ancient monuments include a tall Roman column called Pompey's Pillar. Near the waterfront stand two obelisks, or tall stone towers, called Cleopatra's Needles. Archaeologists are still exploring Alexandria's offshore waters. They have found ruins of ancient treasures such as the Pharos Lighthouse.

Giza (above) is Egypt's third-largest city, with a population of almost 2,700,000. Located southwest of Cairo, on the west bank of the Nile, it is the capital city's largest suburb. Giza is best known as the site of the three great pyramids and the Sphinx. It is also home to the University of Cairo and many museums, embassies, and government offices. Visitors can travel by boat to Pharaonic Village, a living history museum on an island in the Nile.

Shubra al Khaymah is a northern suburb of Cairo. It's Egypt's fourth-largest city, with a population of more than 1,000,000 people. Muhammad Ali Pasha built the city in the 1800s, and his palace is the major tourist site there. Located on the Nile's east bank, Shubra al Khaymah was once a market center for farm products from the Nile Delta. Egypt's first European-style schools and factories were built there in the 1820s. Today, it is an industrial center specializing in textiles, glass, rubber, and other goods.

Passengers on a boat on Lake Nasser get a good look at the Great Temple of Ramses II. The temple was moved to higher ground, so it would not be flooded when the lake was formed.

A large settlement called the Fayyum lies just west of the Nile. Its palm trees, mountains, and ancient ruins are surrounded by desert. But the Fayyum is not really an oasis. Its water supply comes from a tributary, or branch, of the Nile.

Oasis water, rich with sulfur and other minerals, is known for its health benefits. People come from all over the world to bathe in these waters. The silt—particles of sediment that sink to the bottom—is also used to treat bone, skin, muscle, and stomach problems.

Lake Nasser and the Aswan High Dam

Lake Nasser, south of Aswan, is Egypt's largest lake. It stretches for 340 miles (550 km) across Egypt's border into Sudan. Lake Nasser is an artificial lake. It was created in the 1960s when the Aswan High Dam was built across the Nile.

In the 1950s, President Gamal Abdel Nasser decided to build the Aswan High Dam. Waters behind the dam would form a lake, but that presented a problem. The lake would flood ancient monuments such as the temples of Abu Simbel and Philae. Thousands of engineers and laborers from all over the world formed a rescue team to save them. Stone by stone, they moved the monuments to higher ground. This massive project took more than ten years. The Aswan High Dam and its power station began operating in 1970.

Damming the Nile has brought many benefits. It controls Egypt's annual floodwaters, enabling farmers to grow crops year-round, and it makes irrigation easier. Also, water rushing over the dam produces hydroelectric power and improves boat travel on the Nile.

The dam has its drawbacks, though. Silt from the river gets trapped in Lake Nasser. The Nile valley no longer gets that natural fertilizer. The delta has suffered, too. Without the Nile's natural gushing force, saltwater from the Mediterranean creeps upstream. And without steady silt deposits, the Mediterranean coast is eroding, or washing away.

The construction of the Aswan High Dam blocked the flow of the Nile, flooding the nearby land. About one hundred thousand people were forced to move.

The Sinai Peninsula

The Sinai Peninsula is part desert and part rugged mountains. More camel trails than roads cross this region. Bedouin nomads have lived in the Sinai for centuries. Now, vacationers and tourists visit the seaside resort towns that line the Sinai's Mediterranean coast.

Rocky mountain ranges rise in the south. The best-known peaks are Jabal Katrina (Mount Catherine)—Egypt's highest point at 8,668 feet (2,642 m) above sea level—and Jabal Musa (Mountain of Moses or Mount Sinai). At the base of Mount Sinai is Saint Catherine's Greek Orthodox monastery. The Colored Canyon, not far from Mount Sinai, has striped rock formations in shades of pink, orange, and yellow.

Southern Sinai is flanked by two arms of the Red Sea—the Gulf of Suez on the west and the Gulf of Aqaba on the east. Tourists enjoy South Sinai's coastal resort cities. Some are simple towns with thatched-roof waterfront huts, while others offer lavish hotels, restaurants, and entertainment. Snorkeling and scuba diving near the coral reefs are also major attractions. The resort city of Sharm el-Sheikh, on the peninsula's southern tip, was once a small fishing village. Now it's the Sinai's largest city.

Climate

Egypt has two seasons—summer and winter. Summers, from May through October, are sweltering. To escape the heat, many Egyptians head for the cool sea breezes of the Mediterranean coast. Winters—November through April—are mild and

Temperatures in Egypt's deserts often reach 114°F (46°C).

sometimes cool. All year long, temperatures in Upper Egypt are higher than those in the north. Mountainous regions of the Sinai can be quite chilly.

In the desert, the glaring sun makes midday travel dangerous. Travelers on camel often sleep during the hottest part of the day. They travel before mid-morning and after sundown. Nights in the desert can be icy cold, though. That's because sand does not hold on to the sun's heat. In April, desert dwellers take cover during the *khamsin*—a hot, dry wind from the south that causes blinding sandstorms.

Most of Egypt's rain falls in the winter near the Mediterranean. It almost never rains in the desert. Snow is seen only on the Sinai's highest mountaintops, where some 11 inches (28 cm) fall every year.

CHAPTER THREE

Nature in the Desert

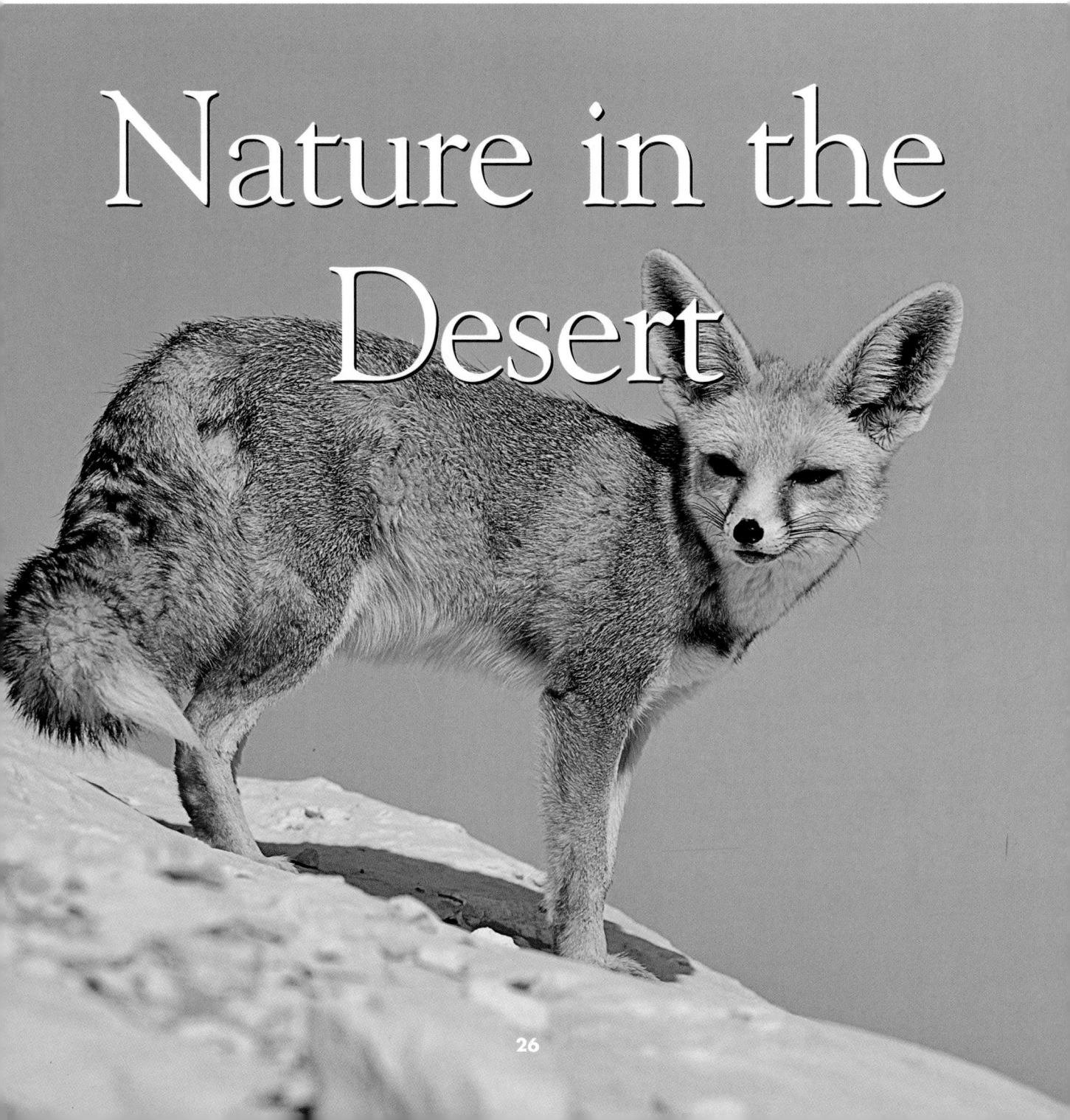

ANCIENT EGYPT SWARMED WITH ANIMALS, especially in the Nile River valley. Hippopotamuses bobbed in the cool Nile waters and lounged along the shore. Lions emerged from the desert to drink at the water's edge. Baboons and wildcats screeched in the thickets, and herds of gazelles trotted by. Golden jackals scoured the valleys for animal and human remains. Great flocks of rose-colored flamingos swooped in to nest along the Nile, and red-breasted geese flew in to winter in the marshes.

As the climate grew hotter and drier, and human settlements spread, some of these animals went away. We know they once lived there because Egyptians left paintings of them. Some animals were honored as gods.

The lions and hippos are gone now, but the Nile valley is still teeming with wildlife. One of the most fearsome river creatures is the Nile crocodile. These meat eaters have powerful jaws, and they sometimes work together to take down much larger animals. Crocodiles were once found all along the

Opposite: **The fennec, a tiny fox, lives in Egypt and other parts of North Africa. Heat leaves the fox's body through its large ears, helping it keep cool in the desert.**

Nile, but since the Aswan High Dam was built, they now live only south of Lake Nasser, so few people see them.

Egypt's temples and pyramids make safe homes for many animals. The monuments shelter animals from the desert heat and provide good hiding places. Colonies of bats cling to the ceilings and walls. The golden spiny mouse sleeps in a dark corner in the daytime and comes out at night. The orange head of the agama, or gray lizard, blends in with the stones.

With its sweltering days and chilly nights, the desert is a rough habitat for animals. Skinks, lizards, and other reptiles can stand these extremes, but some animals, such as hyenas, creep out only at night.

In many ways, hyenas look and behave like dogs, but they are actually more closely related to cats.

The tail of the scorpion ends in a venomous stinger. Only a few scorpion species have venom that is dangerous to humans.

Furry little fennecs are foxes that weigh only about 3 pounds (1.4 kilograms). They're also called desert foxes or sand foxes. Fennecs spend the day in their underground burrows to escape the heat. They come out at night to feed on insects, fruit, and small animals. Their big eyes and long ears help them to locate prey—and predators.

The deserts are also home to plenty of scorpions and snakes. The venomous saw-scaled viper is a relative of the rattlesnake. Its scales make a scratchy sound as it moves across the sand. Sand boas, however, are not dangerous to humans. They help keep down the rodent population and are a protected species.

The ibex, a wild mountain goat with long, curved horns, scampers over steep, rocky slopes in the Sinai. In the daytime, a Sinai rodent called the rock hyrax basks in the sun. At night, it eats acacia plants.

Caracals sometimes jump as high as 10 feet (3 m) to catch birds.

Wildcats

It was in Egypt that cats were first domesticated, or tamed. People keep cats as pets in Egypt today, but many kinds of wildcats still roam the deserts. Wild swamp cats can be seen slinking around in the delta.

The Kaffir cat is also called the Egyptian wildcat. It looks much like a tabby cat, but its tail is longer and thicker. It hunts rodents, birds, and snakes, just as domestic cats do.

Sand cats are wildcats that live in the desert. They're about the size of house cats, and they're built for desert living. Their paws have thick fur on the bottom to protect their feet from the burning sands. Sand cats can live for long periods without drinking water, too. They hunt small rodents, and they get fluids from the bodies of their prey.

Caracals, or desert lynxes, are among Egypt's largest wildcats. Their golden-brown color blends in with the desert sands. Tufts of black hair stick up on the top of their long, pointy ears. Caracals are swift runners. This enables them to pounce on birds, their main prey.

Ships of the Desert

People have used camels to travel through the desert for thousands of years. Camels are sometimes called ships of the desert because they navigate vast oceans of sand. Egypt's nomadic Bedouin people call them *ata Allah*, meaning "God's gift."

These hardy beasts can travel for about a week without eating food or drinking water. Their key to survival is their humps. Camels store fat and fluids in their humps. When food

Built for Endurance

Camels can raise their own body temperature to keep themselves from sweating. They cannot afford to lose fluids in the desert heat. When they have a chance to drink water, they fill up. A camel can drink more than 32 gallons (120 liters) of water without stopping.

A double row of long, curly eyelashes protects a camel's eyes from sand and dust. Broad, leathery foot pads keep its feet from sinking into the sand. Camels have big nostrils, which they can close to keep sand out.

A camel can carry a load as heavy as 500 pounds (225 kg). Usually camels slouch along at about 3 miles (5 km) per hour. But camels bred for racing can gallop as fast as 40 miles (65 km) per hour.

is scarce, they draw energy from the stored fat. Egypt's camels are dromedaries, or one-humped camels. Bactrian camels of Asia have two humps.

Camels have a bad reputation for spitting, kicking, and biting. But their riders don't mind. The camel's gentle, lurching pace is a first-class comfort on long trips.

Birds

Many birds that live near the Nile feed on fish. One is the pied kingfisher. It dives in and snaps up fish with its long bill. Long-legged herons also wade and fish along the Nile.

Ibises are common waterbirds, too. They have powerful legs for wading in the water and long, curved bills for snatching fish. Many kinds of ibis live near the Nile, and the dazzling scarlet ibis is the most spectacular. The ibis has been around since ancient times. It was a symbol of the god Thoth, who appears in ancient Egyptian art with the head of an ibis.

Ibises have long, curved beaks, which they use to search in the mud for food.

The Steppe Eagle

Egypt has no official national animals, but its unofficial animal is the steppe eagle. This large, brown bird favors dry places. It nests in central Asia in the spring and spends its winters in Egypt. Steppe eagles have a huge wingspan, stretching as wide as 80 inches (200 cm). They feed on small birds, mice, and other small rodents. Steppe eagles often steal prey from other predatory birds.

Huge flocks of flamingos swoop down upon the Nile in the winter. Flamingos are known for being pink, but they do not have to be. Flamingos' feathers are naturally white. The feathers take on a pink color as the birds eat tiny pink brine shrimp!

Gulls, ospreys, and spoonbills nest on the Red Sea coast. Lake Nasser is a haven for migrating birds. Pelicans, geese, terns, plovers, and warblers are seen along the shore.

Cattle egrets are common in farming areas. They dip over the fields looking for insects and frogs. Doves, bee-eaters, and black kites live in the countryside as well as the cities. Hoopoes are city birds that cruise grassy patches for insects. Rock martins and white-crowned wheatears build their nests in rocky nooks and crevices.

Life in the Coral Reefs

Coral reefs line the underwater banks of the Red Sea. A coral reef is actually made of skeletons. Tiny animals called coral polyps live in huge colonies along the coast. When the polyps die, new polyps attach themselves to the skeletons.

A silky shark swims above a coral reef in the Red Sea, searching for food.

Generation after generation, millions of skeletons build up to form a massive reef.

The coral reef is home to a rainbow of colorful sea creatures—red sponges, pink organ-pipe sponges, and green sea anemones, as well as prickly sea urchins and feathery fan worms. In and out of this maze swim blue tangs, red groupers, angelfish, butterfly fish, parrotfish, blue and white Napoleon fish, lionfish, surgeonfish, sharks, and moray eels. Inching along the bottom are sea slugs and giant clams.

Plants

As early as 3500 BCE, Egyptians used fibers of the papyrus plant to make writing paper. The plant became so important to their culture that it was used as a hieroglyph, or writing symbol, to represent the delta, or kingdom of Lower Egypt. Today, papyrus is cultivated mainly in the delta region and rarely grows in the wild.

The lotus, a flowering aquatic plant that once grew all along the Nile, was the royal symbol for Upper Egypt. Today, it is found only in the delta, in hidden bends of the Nile, and in the Fayyum.

Tall reeds thrive along the Nile's banks and on its islands. Acacias brighten the riverbanks with their yellow flowers. The water hyacinth, however, is a beautiful, blue-flowered pest. This hardy plant spreads fast and clogs irrigation canals.

The tamarisk shrubs that grow around Lake Nasser and the Sinai ooze a sweet, sticky substance. Herdsmen sell this substance to tourists. Some people believe it's the manna that Israelites ate in the desert in Biblical times.

Date palms grow along the Nile and in the oases along with groves of citrus, pomegranate, and apricot trees. A sharp, aromatic smell is a sign that eucalyptus trees are nearby. Egypt's only forests are the mangrove forests on the coasts of the Red Sea and the southeast Sinai. The roots of saltwater mangrove trees grow partly under the water and partly above the surface.

The National Flower

Egypt's national flower is the Egyptian lotus, also called the Egyptian blue water lily. Ancient Egyptians linked the lotus with the sun. They believed the sun god emerged from the first Egyptian lotus. The lotus opens its petals to follow the sun by day and closes its petals when the sun goes down in the evening. As a sacred plant, the lotus was carved at the top of many Egyptian temple columns. People also used lotus petals for their healing properties.

CHAPTER

FOUR

From Pharaohs to Presidents

EGYPT'S LONG HISTORY BEGINS MORE THAN SEVEN thousand years ago. People were farming along the Nile as early as 5000 BCE. Eventually, they settled into two kingdoms—Upper Egypt in the south, and Lower Egypt in the northern delta. In about 3100 BCE, Menes, a king of Upper Egypt, united the two kingdoms. Menes was honored as Egypt's first *pharaoh*, or king. The word *pharaoh* comes from the words *per 'aa*, meaning "big house."

Opposite: **Tutankhamen was pharaoh in the fourteenth century BCE. This image of Tutankhamen and his queen decorated his throne.**

Pharaohs liked to keep their power in the family. Ancient Egypt was governed by one dynasty, or ruling family, after another. Thirty dynasties of pharaohs reigned in Egypt between 3100 BCE and 332 BCE.

Ancient Egyptian Society

The pharaoh and his family were at the top rung of Egyptian society. They lived in great luxury. Alabaster lamps, golden beds and chairs, and exotic woods inlaid with ivory decorated their homes. Servants took care of their every need. Musicians and dancers amused guests at their lavish banquets. Other members of the upper class were priests, nobles, doctors, and high-ranking army officers.

Artisans, merchants, and engineers made up the middle class. Scribes, or professional writers, held a special place of honor. Every family hoped to have a son who would become a scribe. The scribes wrote letters and government documents and recorded the pharaohs' decrees.

The common people were farmers, laborers, and soldiers. Farming took only part of the year, so many farmers spent several months working on the pharaohs' construction projects.

Women in ancient Egypt had more rights than many women of the time. They could own property, buy and sell goods, and inherit wealth. Wives could even sue for divorce if they had a good reason.

This painting from about 3,500 years ago shows Egyptians cultivating wheat.

The Cycle of Floods

Ancient Egyptians divided the year into three seasons of four months each. The new year began with the flooding of the Nile in July. This was the season of *akhet*. In November, as the waters receded, *peret*—the plowing and planting season—began. The dry season, *shemu*, lasted from March to July. Then crops were harvested and stored before the rains came again.

The floodwaters left a deposit of silt that fertilized the fields and produced abundant crops. Mud along the riverbank was made into pots, jars, tiles, and other ceramics. People measured the rise and fall of the Nile's water level with a *nilometer*—a series of marks on riverside rocks or cliffs.

This vase with a horse design dates back about 3,500 years.

Farmers produced more than enough food for Egypt's people. The pharaohs' storehouses brimmed over with the food they collected as taxes. Egypt was able to trade grain and other crops with neighboring peoples in Africa and Asia.

Hieroglyphs

Egyptians were writing with picture symbols called hieroglyphs as early as 3000 BCE. Some symbols stood for sounds. Others showed whether a word was singular or plural, or a noun or a verb. By 300 BCE, the Egyptian alphabet consisted or more than seven hundred hieroglyphic symbols.

Some hieroglyphic symbols stand for sounds, and some stand for words.

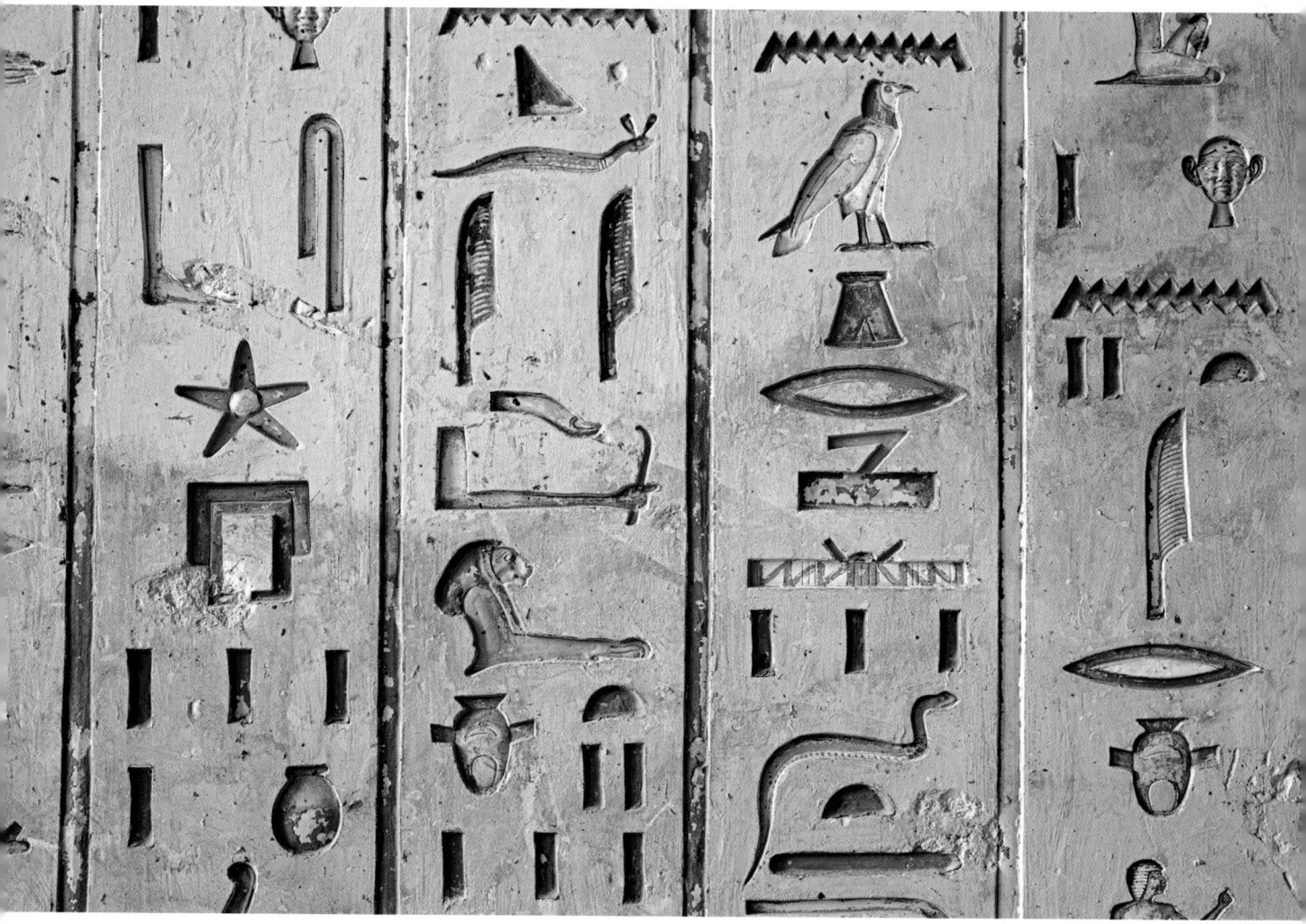

A massive statue of Amon-Re sits at Karnak. He was considered the king of the Egyptian gods.

Religious Beliefs

Ancient Egyptians worshipped many gods and goddesses. They believed their gods caused the sun to rise, the Nile to flood, the crops to grow, and the cows to give milk. Each town and family had its own special gods. The pharaoh himself was seen as a god who protected the people.

Priests took care of the temples and made offerings at the proper times. Re, the sun god, was the most important of all the gods. Amon, the sun god of Thebes, was combined with Re as Amon-Re. His temple at Karnak, near Luxor, was a great center of worship for hundreds of years. One pharaoh after another built additions onto the temple until it covered a huge area.

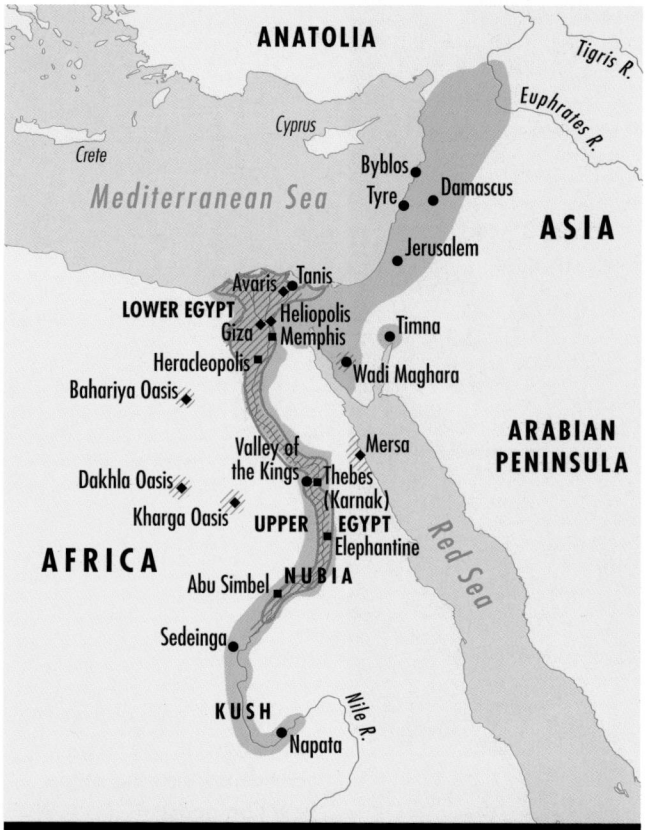

Ancient Egypt

- Old Kingdom, ca. 2575 BCE –2130 BCE
- Middle Kingdom, ca. 2040 BCE –1630 BCE
- New Kingdom, ca. 1540 BCE –1075 BCE
- Old Kingdom sites
- Middle Kingdom sites
- New Kingdom sites

The age of 110 was believed to be the perfect life span, but it was more an ideal than a reality. Most people in those days did not live past their thirties. But every Egyptian, from pharaoh to laborer, believed in life after death. Given the proper burial rites, they could be immortal.

The Egyptians believed that the jackal-headed god Anubis escorted each soul into the afterlife. Osiris, god of the underworld, made a final judgment by the "weighting of the heart." A feather was put on one side of a scale, and the person's heart on the other side. If the heart was as light as the feather, the soul could enter eternity.

Egyptians also believed that the dead would enjoy all their earthly comforts in the afterlife. Burial chambers were filled with favorite possessions, clothes, furniture, games, and food. Even pet cats were preserved and buried with their masters.

The Pyramids

To make sure they would have eternal life, pharaohs built fabulous tombs for themselves. The earliest pharaohs built tombs called mastabas—low, flat-topped, mud-brick structures with slanting sides. Djoser, a pharaoh of the Third Dynasty, wanted a more glorious tomb, so his architect, Imhotep, built the first pyramid. It is called a step pyramid because its sides are like stair steps. Djoser's Step Pyramid still stands at Saqqara, near Memphis.

Fourth Dynasty pharaohs built the most famous pyramids—the three pyramids of Giza, just west of Cairo. Khufu built the largest one, called the Great Pyramid, around 2500 BCE. It was made of limestone blocks covered with sheer granite slabs that glistened in the sun. In later centuries, the granite was removed to make buildings in Cairo. Khufu's son Khafre and the pharaoh Menkaure built the two other Giza

The Great Pyramid of Giza

Pharaoh Khufu built the Great Pyramid as a monumental tomb for himself and his queen. Narrow passageways inside the pyramid lead to their burial chambers. At the time, the Great Pyramid was the largest building in the world. Its square base measures 756 feet (230 m) on each side. That's more than twice as long as an American football field. The pyramid stands 481 feet (147 m) high—almost as tall as a fifty-story building. It was constructed with more than two million stone blocks, averaging 2.5 tons apiece.

The ancient Egyptians left only a few clues about how they built the pyramids. From rock quarries at Aswan, workers floated stone blocks down the Nile on rafts for 500 miles (800 km). Then the blocks were probably put on runners, like sleds, and hauled up wooden or stone ramps.

The Great Sphinx is 241 feet (74 m) long.

pyramids. Nearby stands the Great Sphinx, a massive stone lion with the head of a human.

Kingdoms Unite and Divide

The history of ancient Egypt can be divided into three major periods—the Old Kingdom, the Middle Kingdom, and the New Kingdom. Memphis was Egypt's capital during the Old Kingdom period, beginning around 2575 BCE. (Memphis lies a few miles south of what is now Cairo.) In time, the pharaohs' power weakened, and Egypt once again broke into separate districts. Mentuhotep II pulled the kingdom together again. He built his capital at Thebes, on the Nile's east bank in Upper Egypt. His reign marks the beginning of the Middle Kingdom period. During this time, construction began on the Temple of Amon at Karnak.

Major Periods in Ancient Egyptian History

ca. 3100 BCE	Menes unites Upper and Lower Egypt
ca. 2925 BCE–ca. 2575 BCE	Early dynastic period
ca. 2575 BCE–ca. 2130 BCE	Old Kingdom
1938 BCE–ca. 1630 BCE	Middle Kingdom
ca. 1539 BCE–1075 BCE	New Kingdom
323 BCE–30 BCE	Ptolemaic period

The New Kingdom: Conquests and Construction

Ahmose, a Theban prince, introduced the New Kingdom period, with Thebes as the capital. Hatshepsut, a female pharaoh, ruled for twenty-two years during this time. Egypt soon became a major world power. Under Hatshepsut's stepson, Thutmose III, Egypt took over Nubia, Palestine, Syria, and northern Iraq. New lands meant new sources of wealth. Slaves, exotic woods, ivory, and precious metals and stones poured into the pharaohs' warehouses. A later pharaoh, Tutankhamen, was known as the boy king. Commonly known as King Tut, he died in 1352 BCE when he was about eighteen years old. His lavish tomb contained thousands of objects intended for his use in the afterlife.

The gold burial mask of Tutankhamen is now in the Cairo Museum.

To show off their power, New Kingdom pharaohs built huge temples, monuments, and statues of themselves. Ramses II was the greatest builder of all. He built the temples at Abu Simbel and enlarged the temple at Karnak. For their tombs, New Kingdom rulers built huge necropolises, or cities of the dead. These tomb sites were on the west bank of the Nile, across from Thebes. Today, they are named the Valley of the Kings, the Valley of the Queens, and the Tombs of the Nobles.

Ramses III of the Twentieth Dynasty was the last great New Kingdom pharaoh. In later dynasties, foreigners from Nubia,

Passageways lead into various tombs in the Valley of the Kings. The site includes sixty-three separate tombs.

Egyptians welcomed Alexander the Great and his troops when they entered Egypt in 332 BCE.

Libya, Ethiopia, and Assyria held the throne. Cambyses, the son of Persia's Cyrus the Great, invaded Egypt in 525 BCE, and Persian pharaohs ruled for the next two hundred years.

Alexander and the Ptolemies

In 332 BCE, Alexander the Great marched into Egypt. Just twenty-four years old, he already ruled the Greek Empire. Now he was helping to disband the Persian Achaemenian Empire. Egyptians were glad to have Alexander deliver them from the Persians. In Memphis, he was enthroned as pharaoh. He built his capital city on the Mediterranean coast and named it Alexandria. Alexander also paid a visit to the famous oracle, or fortune-teller, at Siwa. Rumors said the oracle declared Alexander a god.

Ptolemy was a childhood friend of Alexander's and one of his most trusted generals.

Before he died in 323 BCE, Alexander divided his empire among his finest generals. Egypt went to Ptolemy, who installed himself as pharaoh. The Ptolemies reigned for the next three hundred years. During the Ptolemaic period, Egypt was drenched in Greek culture. Greek scholars and scientists made Alexandria the cultural capital of the Mediterranean. Astronomers, mathematicians, doctors, and engineers worked and studied there. Alexandria's library and museum had the most magnificent collection of manuscripts and documents in the world.

Across the Mediterranean Sea from Egypt, another great empire was on the rise. The Roman Empire was spreading across southern Europe and into Asia. Naturally, the Romans turned their eyes to Egypt. For years, the Ptolemies, including Cleopatra, the last Ptolemy ruler, paid exorbitant taxes to Rome. Cleopatra had a plan for preventing the Roman Empire from taking over Egypt.

Cleopatra believed her best chance to save her kingdom was to join forces with Rome. She befriended Julius Caesar, the Roman emperor, and they had a son. After Caesar was assassinated, she married one of his generals, Mark Antony. The marriage suited Mark Antony's ambitions, too. With his forces and Egypt's combined, he could defeat his rival, Octavian, and rule the whole Roman Empire.

Unfortunately for the wedded couple, things did not work out as they had planned. Octavian conquered Egypt's forces at the sea battle of Actium in 31 BCE. He captured Alexandria the following year. Seeing that they had lost everything, Mark Antony and Cleopatra committed suicide, and Egypt became a Roman province. The days of the pharaohs were over.

Mark Antony tells Cleopatra about a victory over Octavian. In the end, however, Octavian's forces triumphed.

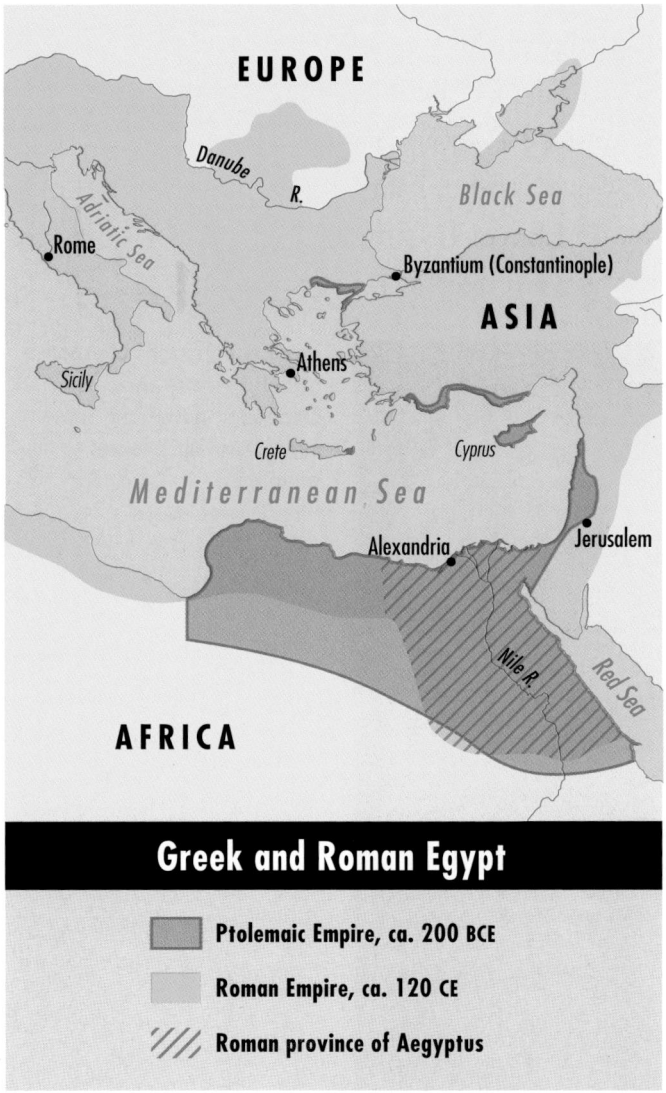

Roman Rule

Life was rough for Egyptians under Roman rule. The Roman governors demanded huge taxes and forced Egyptian peasants to serve in the Roman army. Loads of grain from Egypt's farms were shipped to Rome.

In the first century CE, Christianity sprang up in the Roman Empire. In Egypt, the Christian community was known as the Coptic Church. Seeing the new religion as a threat, Roman emperors outlawed it and began executing Christians. In the third century CE, Emperor Diocletian had thousands of Egypt's Christians put to death. Later emperors reversed the rule. In 313, Emperor Constantine converted to Christianity, and later Theodosius made it the Roman Empire's official religion.

In 395, the Roman Empire split in two. Rome was the capital of the Western Empire, and the Eastern, or Byzantine, Empire was ruled from Constantinople (now Istanbul, Turkey). Egypt became part of the Byzantine Empire. As the Byzantines weakened, Egypt became ripe for another takeover.

The Arab Invasion

Across the Red Sea in Arabia, Muhammad (ca. 570–632) was preaching the new religion of Islam. Muhammad's teachings spread like wildfire. His followers, called Muslims, waged holy wars across Arabia and north into Syria and Iran. In 639, the Arab army under Amr ibn al-As invaded Egypt, taking Cairo in 641 and Alexandria in 642. Amr ibn al-As built the walled military city of al-Fustat (Old Cairo) in 641.

Eighteen hundred years ago, most people in Egypt were Coptic Christians. This page from a Coptic Bible is from about 400 CE.

Gradually, Arabic ways mixed with local customs or replaced them altogether. The native Coptic language gave way to Arabic as Egypt's official tongue. Islam became the official religion, and the ancient cultures of the pharaohs, Persians, Greeks, and Romans all but disappeared.

The Pharos Lighthouse of Alexandria was considered one of the Seven Wonders of the Ancient World. Built around 280 BCE, it stood about 400 feet (120 m) high.

The First Caliphs

After Muhammad's death, military and religious leaders, called caliphs, ruled Islamic lands. One after another, they fought for control of Muslim territory. At first, Egypt became a province under the Umayyad caliphs (661–750). Their capital was Damascus, in Syria. Abbasid caliphs took over Egypt in 750. They ruled their empire from Baghdad, in present-day Iraq.

Meanwhile, the Fatimid dynasty ruled Tunisia, a North African land west of Egypt. The Fatimid general Jawhar occupied Egypt in 969. Caliph al-Mu'izz built al-Qahirah (Cairo), a new walled city near earlier settlements, in 973, and made it his capital. From there, he overpowered Arabia, Palestine, and Syria.

Egypt prospered under the Fatimids. Merchant ships from India and China brought goods to Alexandria and the

Saladin, the Great Uniter

Saladin is one of the most famous warriors in history. His Arabic name, Salah ad-Din, means "the bounty of religion." As a young man, Saladin studied religion in Damascus. Later he fought against the crusaders in Egypt. Saladin's greatest goal was to drive the crusaders out of Palestine and reunite Muslim lands. In 1171, he ousted the Fatimids and established the Ayyubid dynasty. He went on to capture Jerusalem in 1187 and drove the crusaders to a few coastal towns. Saladin eventually became sultan of Egypt, Syria, Yemen, and Palestine.

Red Sea ports. Egypt then traded those goods with cities in Italy. Al-Azhar University was founded for Shi'i Islamic studies. Arts and literature flourished, and Cairo became a center of learning.

As Islam spread, the Catholic Church watched lands it considered holy being taken over. Pope Urban II, head of the Church, called upon Christians everywhere to fight Crusades, or holy wars, to gain control of these lands. Crusaders focused on Jerusalem, in Palestine, and other places they regarded as holy. In the 1100s, crusaders marched against the Fatimids in Egypt. That paved the way for the Fatimids to fall to Saladin. This great warrior drove out the crusaders, united Muslim lands, and established the Ayyubid dynasty.

The Mamelukes

Ayyubid rulers surrounded themselves with a bevy of soldier-bodyguards called Mamelukes. The first Mamelukes were

A Mameluke horseman in Egypt. Many Mamelukes were skilled military leaders and soldiers.

slaves from Turkey, Greece, and central Asia. They were taken as boys and trained to be soldiers and government officials. Once their training was over, they were free. Some held high positions and became very powerful.

In 1250, the Mamelukes took control of Egypt. Their greatest leader was Baybars, a general who became the fourth Mameluke sultan, or ruler. Baybars drove Mongol invaders out of Palestine, took over Syria, and won many towns away from the crusaders.

Mameluke merchants carried on trade with Europe and Asia. With their vast wealth, they supported the making of beautiful architecture, fine ceramics, and metalwork. In time, however, the Mameluke army split into rival groups and lost its fighting edge.

Ottoman Rule

Selim, a sultan of the Turkish Ottoman Empire, knew his well-equipped army had an unbeatable weapon—newly invented cannons. Selim seized Cairo in 1517, installing himself as caliph.

Egypt remained a province of the Ottoman Empire for almost three hundred years. While Ottoman caliphs ruled in Cairo, Mamelukes served as local administrators. They and the Ottomans struggled for power in Egypt for more than two hundred years.

Napoléon and the French

Napoléon Bonaparte of France sailed a fleet of ships to Egypt's coast on July 1, 1798. France was about to take over much of western Europe, and Great Britain was one of France's greatest enemies. Napoléon wanted to seize Egypt in order to disrupt British trade with the Middle East. In the Battle of the Pyramids near Cairo, Napoléon conquered the Mameluke army and took control of Egypt. He organized a modern government, started irrigation projects, and planned a Suez canal route. French scholars and scientists studied Egypt's culture and farming practices. Archaeologists began to uncover ancient Egypt's buried treasures.

In 1799, Napoléon returned to France, leaving his generals to keep order. Now Great Britain saw its chance to get a foothold in Egypt. British troops joined forces with the Ottomans and Mamelukes. Together, they hammered away at the French until the French pulled out in 1801.

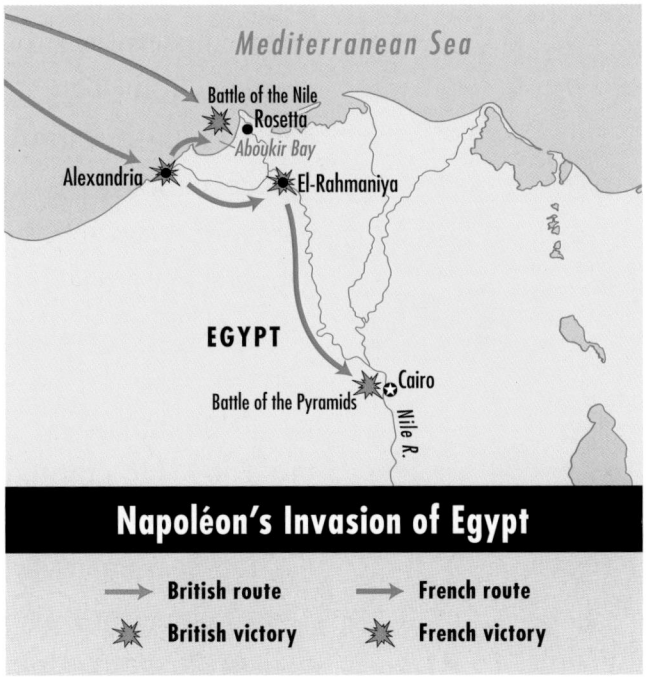

The Rosetta Stone

In 1799, near the Egyptian town of Rosetta, a French officer discovered a slab of stone inscribed with three sets of strange writing. One was hieroglyphic symbols, but no one knew how to read them. The slab, named the Rosetta Stone, went to a museum. Finally, in 1822, Jean-François Champollion cracked the mystery. Two of the inscriptions were in languages that he knew—Greek and demotic, a later form of Egyptian writing. To his surprise, the inscriptions said the same thing. By comparing the hieroglyphs to the other two writings, he developed a "dictionary" for hieroglyphic symbols.

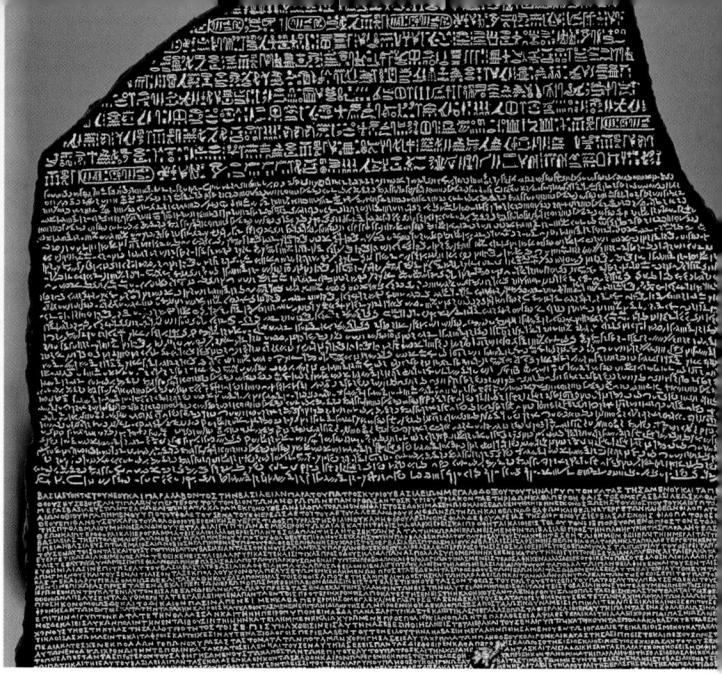

Muhammad Ali: Modernizing Egypt

Egypt's Ottoman governor Muhammad Ali wanted to ensure that he stayed in power. So when he took office in 1805, he set to work modernizing the country, in an effort to prevent European nations from stepping in. He brought in French military advisers to train his army. Factories were built to make textiles and process iron. Schools of medicine and engineering were opened, and European scholars came to lecture. Bright young Egyptians studied in Europe, then came back and translated their textbooks into Arabic. For all his innovations, Muhammad Ali came to be known as the father of modern Egypt.

Muhammad Ali's son, Said Pasha, ruled Egypt from 1854 to 1863. He granted a French company the right to build a canal from the Mediterranean to the Gulf of Suez. Although a French company was in charge, it was Egyptians who did the hard, dangerous work of building the canal. The Suez Canal opened to traffic in 1869.

Said's nephew Ismail improved Egypt's schools, roads, railroads, and factories. But his lavish spending on palaces and other luxuries cast Egypt deep into debt. In 1875, to raise money, Ismail sold Egypt's shares in the Suez Canal to Great Britain. That made France and Britain the canal's primary owners.

British Rule

Fed up with foreigners, Egyptians revolted in 1882. But British forces subdued the rebels and occupied the country. When World War I (1914–1918) broke out, the British declared Egypt a protectorate. This implied that the British were protecting Egypt. In reality, they were protecting the Suez Canal.

In 1922, the British granted independence to Egypt but continued to run much of the country's affairs. The British army stayed during World War II (1939–1945), again to protect the canal. In 1942, German and Italian forces landed on Egypt's Mediterranean coast. At the Battle of El Alamein, which lasted two weeks, British general Bernard Montgomery forced German field marshal Erwin Rommel into retreat.

After the war, the United Nations divided Palestine to make a homeland for Jewish people. Egypt and other Arab countries protested, but the Jewish state of Israel became a reality in 1948. Conflict between Israel and the Arab states continues to this day.

The Nasser Years

After centuries of outside rule, Egyptians were ready to take control of their own country. On July 23, 1952, army officers led by Lieutenant Colonel Gamal Abdel Nasser overthrew

King Farouk reviews troops in 1936.

King Farouk, who had been the ruler of Egypt since 1936. Egypt was declared a republic in 1953. Nasser became prime minister the next year, and the British removed their forces from Egypt. In 1956, Nasser won the presidency.

President Nasser tried to solve many of the problems that troubled his country. He urged rural people to stay in their villages and affirm their Egyptian identity. New laws gave more peasants a chance to own land. Public schools were improved, and graduates were given government jobs.

Nasser planned to build the Aswan High Dam, but he needed money to do it. The United States, Britain, and the

World Bank at first agreed to lend the money. Later, they withdrew the offer. In 1956, Nasser responded by taking control of the Suez Canal, a move that made him a hero in the Arab world. Nasser then took over Egypt's banks and private industries. Nearly 250,000 foreigners were required to leave the country.

Meanwhile, Israelis and Arabs were in constant conflict. In June 1967, Egypt closed the Gulf of Aqaba to Israeli ships. Israel then stormed into several Arab countries, including Egypt, and occupied some of their lands. This is known as the Six-Day War. Israel's victory only increased the Arab states' harsh feelings for Israel.

Sadat and Middle East Peace

After President Nasser's death in 1970, Anwar el-Sadat became president. He reopened Egypt's doors to foreign businesses to help the economy, but Sadat's main concern was Israel.

Father of the Egyptian Republic

Gamal Abdel Nasser (1918–1970) is known as the father of the Egyptian Republic. As an army officer, he led the revolution of 1952 that overthrew King Farouk. Then Egypt became a republic. Nasser became prime minister of the new republic in 1954 and served as president from 1956 to 1970. As president, he introduced a new constitution that granted women the vote and led the country through the Suez Canal crisis and the Six-Day War.

Anwar el-Sadat

Anwar el-Sadat (1918–1981) was Egypt's president from 1970 to 1981. He shared the 1978 Nobel Peace Prize with Israeli prime minister Menachem Begin. The two had signed the 1978 Camp David Accords, which led to the 1979 Egypt–Israel peace treaty. Sadat tried to improve Egypt's economy, but without great success. Many Egyptians became discontent with economic hardships and the Israeli peace treaty. In 1981, Muslim extremists killed Sadat as he watched a military parade commemorating the 1973 October War.

In October 1973, Sadat sent troops across the Suez Canal in an effort to win back the Sinai, which was occupied by Israel. In eighteen days of fighting, called the October War, not much was accomplished. Hoping to make peace, Sadat visited Israeli prime minister Menachem Begin in 1977. The following year, Sadat and Begin met in the United States and signed the Camp David Accords. The two shared the 1978 Nobel Peace Prize for their efforts. The following year, the longtime enemies signed a peace treaty, and Sinai was restored to Egypt.

In October 1981, Sadat was assassinated while he stood on a public platform. The assassins were members of al-Jihad, a Muslim fundamentalist group. Vice President Hosni Mubarak became president.

Mubarak and the Revolution

Like Sadat, President Mubarak took an active role in the Middle East peace process. He called together many peace conferences of Middle Eastern leaders. At home, Mubarak made economic reforms. He began moving the country toward privatization—that is, turning government-run businesses over to private ownership. Few Egyptians benefited from these changes, however.

Mubarak believed that Egypt should have a secular, open society. This conflicted with the strict Muslim views of Islamic fundamentalist groups. They carried out bomb attacks in Cairo and Luxor in 1997, killing dozens of people. Mubarak responded with crackdowns on terrorist leaders and organizations.

Mubarak's friendship with the United States was unpopular with many Egyptians. They opposed both the U.S. alliance with Israel and U.S. actions in the Arab world. The United States' invasion of Iraq in 2003 brought on a wave of demonstrations in Egypt.

Mubarak kept a tight grip on his power and cracked down hard on anyone who challenged his authority. Free elections, freedom of speech, and freedom of the press were unheard-of. In time, even moderate Egyptians came to oppose Mubarak. He finally agreed to hold free and open elections in 2005, but many believed his victory was rigged.

Tensions came to a boiling point in early 2011, when hundreds of thousands of protesters gathered in Cairo's Tahrir Square. Mubarak resigned as president. Military officials stepped in to run the country temporarily, promising democratic elections and numerous reforms. Egyptians looked forward to this new era after their long and rocky history.

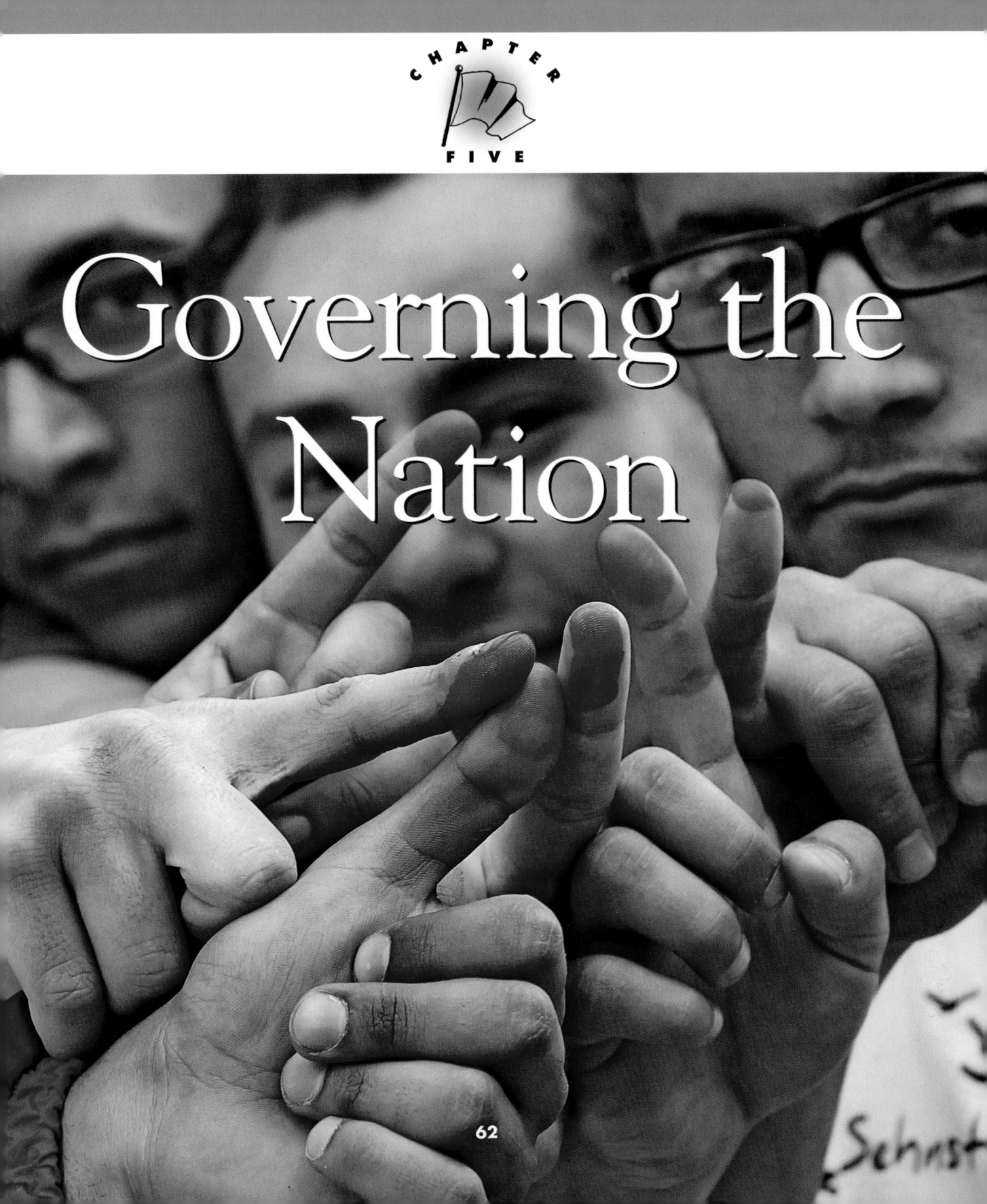
CHAPTER
FIVE
Governing the Nation
Schnst

EGYPT'S OFFICIAL NAME IS THE ARAB REPUBLIC OF Egypt. Like the United States and Canada, Egypt has three branches of government. The president is head of the executive branch. The People's Assembly and the Shura Council are the two houses of Egypt's parliament. It is the nation's legislative, or lawmaking, branch. Egypt's court system makes up the judicial branch.

Egypt has had several constitutions through the years. The 1971 constitution was in effect for forty years. After the 2011 revolution, the military government suspended that constitution and put a temporary one in its place. In March 2011, citizens voted on the reforms they wanted in their new constitution. The changes included limiting a president to two four-year terms and requiring a president to appoint a deputy, or vice president, after taking office. Other provisions make it easier for someone to run for president, make sure that elections are supervised, and make it harder to maintain a state of emergency. These provisions were aimed at eliminating some of the president's abuses of power in the past.

Opposite: **Egyptians display their ink-stained fingers, which show that they voted in the 2011 election on changes to the national constitution.**

The National Flag

Egypt's flag features three horizontal bands—red, white, and black. These are traditional colors for Arabic people. In the center of the white band is the crest of Saladin, the national emblem. It is a golden eagle and shield with a scroll underneath. The red band represents Egypt's history before it became a republic. White stands for Egypt's peaceful revolution in 1952, and black stands for the end of the Egyptian people's oppression. The flag was adopted in 1984.

Election Reforms

"Dead people will not vote in upcoming elections." That was the promise of a government minister as Egypt's 2011 elections drew near. Mubarak's supporters had used many ways to increase votes for their party. Signing dead people's names on the voter lists was just one method. Egypt's electoral process has gone through many stages in the effort to make its elections free, open, and honest.

For many years, the president was chosen by the People's Assembly. At least one-third of the legislators nominated a candidate for president, and two-thirds of the members voted their support. Then the people approved the candidate in a referendum. This system assured that the president would always belong to the majority party.

The electoral system began to come under fire in the late 1990s, however. Egypt's leading political party—the National Democratic Party (NDP)—held a vast majority in the People's Assembly. It seemed that President Hosni Mubarak, the party

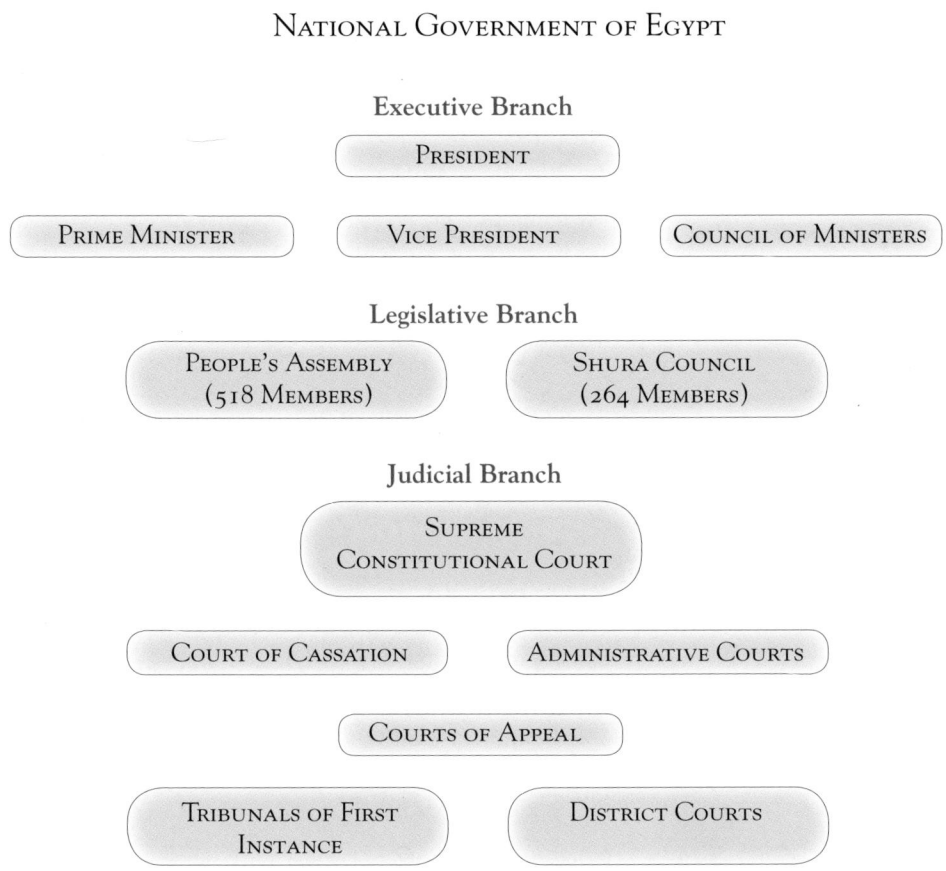

leader who took office in 1981, would be president forever.

In 2005, the constitution was amended to change the electoral process. The amendment paved the way for candidates of many parties to run for president and for voters to elect the president by a direct vote. Egyptians welcomed these measures as a step toward democracy. However, Mubarak's landslide reelection seemed to show that the people's votes were not counted properly. Election reforms after the 2011 revolution promised to bring real change to the electoral system.

The National Anthem

The words to Egypt's national anthem, "*Biladi, Biladi, Biladi*" ("My Homeland, My Homeland, My Homeland"), are by Younis-al Qadi, and the music is by Sayed Darwish. Egypt adopted the anthem in 1979.

Arabic lyrics	**English translation**
Biladi, biladi, biladi	My homeland, my homeland, my homeland,
Laki hubbi wa fu'adi.	My love and my heart are for thee.
Biladi biladi biladi	My homeland, my homeland, my homeland,
Laki hubbi wa fu'adi.	My love and my heart are for thee.
Misr ya umm al-bilad	Egypt! O mother of all lands,
Anti ghayati wal-murad	My hope and my ambition,
Wa 'ala kull al-'ibad	How can one count
Kam linelik min ayad.	The blessings of the Nile for mankind?
Misr inti aghla durra	Egypt! Most precious jewel,
Fawq gabeen ad-dahr ghurra	Shining on the brow of eternity!
Ya biladi 'aishi hurra	O my homeland, be forever free,
Wa as 'adi ragh-al-adi.	Safe from every foe!
Misr awladik kiram	Egypt! Noble are thy children,
Aufiya yar'u-ziman	Loyal, and guardians of thy soil.
Saufa takhti bil-maram	In war and peace
Bittihadhim wa-ittihadi.	We give our lives for thy sake.

The Executive Branch

Egypt's president is the chief executive and head of state. He sets government policies and commands the armed forces. The president is required to appoint one or more vice presidents. He also appoints a prime minister and a council of ministers. The president chooses many local officials, too. An Egyptian president must be a man born of Egyptian parents, be at least forty years old, and be married to an Egyptian woman.

The People's Assembly and the Shura Council

The People's Assembly is the lower house of Egypt's parliament. It handles day-to-day lawmaking. The entire People's Assembly is elected at one time, and its members serve a five-year term. Traditionally, the assembly had a total of 454 members, at least half of who must come from the laborer and farmer classes. The president appointed ten of the members. The

The duties of the People's Assembly include passing laws, approving treaties, and approving the budget.

other 444 were elected by popular vote, with two members from each of 222 districts. In 2009, the number of assembly members was increased to 518, with the extra 64 seats going to women candidates.

The 264-member Shura Council is the upper house of parliament. It studies national issues and drafts proposals and laws. It also advises the president and the People's Assembly, although it has no lawmaking power. The president appoints one-third of its members, and voters elect the others. Shura Council members serve six-year terms.

After the 2011 revolution, the military government dissolved Egypt's parliament. New parliamentary elections were scheduled for late 2011.

Members of the Shura Council must approve all changes to the constitution.

The Courts

The Supreme Constitutional Court is Egypt's highest court. Its judges review the laws to make sure they are in line with the constitution. They also resolve conflicts between lower courts. When two courts make opposite decisions, the Supreme Court makes a ruling.

There are two types of lower courts: courts of general jurisdiction and administrative courts. The highest court of general jurisdiction is the court of cassation. It hears disputed cases from courts of appeal. Below the courts of appeal are tribunals of first instance and district courts. Each of these is divided into civil and criminal chambers. Administrative courts handle lawsuits against the government and its agencies. Judges decide all court cases in Egypt. There are no trials by jury.

Islam is Egypt's national religion, but freedom of worship is guaranteed for people of other faiths. Legal questions concerning marriage and family are decided by the religious law of the people involved. For most Egyptians, this is Islamic law. Christians and Jews resolve these problems within their own religious communities.

Local Government

Egypt is divided into twenty-seven *muhafazat*, or governorates. These divisions are like U.S. states or Canadian provinces. The national government appoints a governor to each governorate. A few of the governorates, such as Cairo and Alexandria, are actually large cities.

The Capital City

Cairo, Egypt's capital, is the largest city in Egypt, with a population of 6,758,581 in 2006. More than 18 million people are packed into the Cairo area, making it the largest metropolitan area in Africa. It is also one of the world's most densely populated areas. Cairo straddles the Nile River and includes two islands—Gezira and Roda. Bridges connect the riverbanks and the islands. Even on a quick tour through the Cairo area, a visitor sees monuments from five thousand years of Egypt's history.

The most modern sections of Cairo lie close to the Nile. Near the east bank is the main business section, as well as the Egyptian Museum and the Mugama'a, or government building. The Opera House/Cultural Center and the 614-foot (187 m) Cairo Tower stand on Gezira Island. To the northeast, a huge statue of Ramses II towers over the main railway station.

East of the city center is Khan al-Khalili souq, or market. Merchants have sold their wares there since the Fatimid dynasty in the 900s. South of the market are some of Egypt's grandest Islamic sites, including the Ottoman mosque of Muhammad Ali, Saladin's Citadel, and the madrasa (religious school) of Mameluke Sultan Hassan.

Old Cairo, to the south, is the oldest section of town. It contains the Roman Fort of Babylon, the Coptic Museum, and many Coptic Christian churches. Looming west of Cairo are the pyramids of Giza. They are close enough to be seen clearly from the windows of many Cairo office buildings.

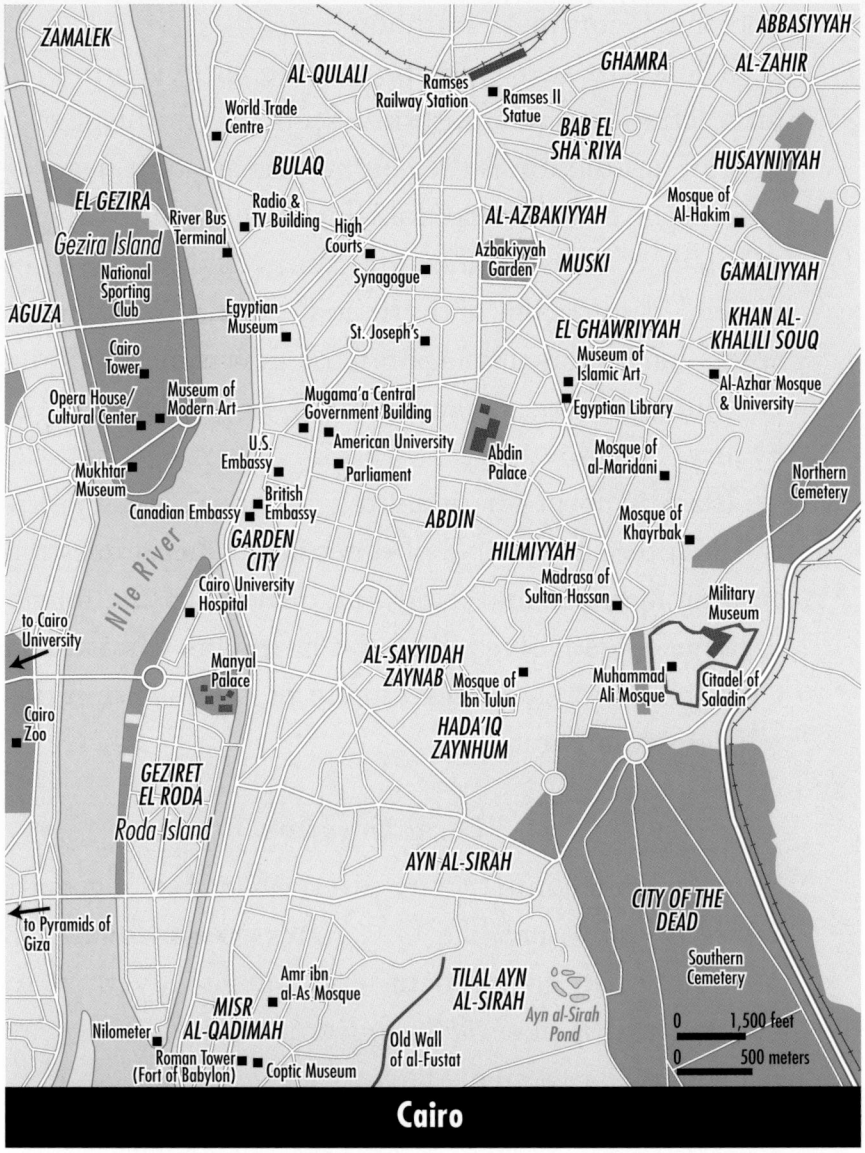

Cairo

Each governorate is divided into districts. Within most districts are towns and villages, each with a mayor and local councils. The local councils oversee education, health care, housing, farming, and many other activities in the community.

Political Parties

Political parties were outlawed in 1953, but the ban was lifted in 1977. By 2005, there were more than a dozen official parties. The National Democratic Party (NDP) was Egypt's major political party from its founding in 1978 until it was dissolved in 2011. Its members typically held the majority of seats in the People's Assembly, and the party leader was Egypt's president.

By law, no party can be based solely on religious issues. That eliminates Egypt's Islamic fundamentalist groups, or Islamists. They want to reshape Egypt as an Islamic society ruled by Islamic law. But one of these groups, the Muslim Brotherhood (MB), has made headway in the political system.

Formed in 1928, the MB was banned in 1954. But it found ways to gain power over the years. In some elections, the

Boutros Boutros-Ghali

Boutros Boutros-Ghali (1922–) was secretary-general of the United Nations from 1992 to 1996. He led the UN during several international crises: the breakup of Yugoslavia, the genocide in Rwanda, and the civil war in Angola. Born in Cairo, Boutros-Ghali is a Coptic Christian.

Brotherhood won seats in the People's Assembly by forming alliances with approved parties. Many more members won seats by running as independents.

Meanwhile, a split was emerging within the Brotherhood. Some members favored a conservative outlook. Others wanted to enter fully into Egypt's political life and push for govern-

The Egyptian government has sometimes arrested people for belonging to the Muslim Brotherhood. Here, protesters demonstrate against these arrests.

Mohamed ElBaradei

Mohamed ElBaradei (1942–) was director general of the International Atomic Energy Agency (IAEA) from 1997 to 2009. The IAEA is an agency of the United Nations devoted to the peaceful use of nuclear energy. In 2002, ElBaradei carried out inspections in Iraq to find evidence of a nuclear program but found none. He and the IAEA were awarded the 2005 Nobel Peace Prize for their efforts to prevent nuclear warfare. ElBaradei played a leading role in opposing Hosni Mubarak's regime and became a leader in the 2011 Egyptian revolution. He also planned to run for president in the post-revolution elections.

ment reforms along with other dissatisfied Egyptians. This made the MB a real threat to Mubarak's power. Government crackdowns led to the arrests of hundreds of MB members. Nevertheless, MB candidates won 88 seats in the 2005 elections and became the largest group opposing the NDP. The MB also had a strong voice in the 2011 revolution. Afterward, MB leaders announced the formation of the Freedom and Justice Party. An April 2011 poll found that around 75 percent of Egyptians had a positive view of the MB. However, only 17 percent thought the MB should lead Egypt's government.

Other parties include the New Wafd Party, the National Progressive Unionist Party, and the al-Ghad Party. All favor some version of political reforms. Candidates from these and several other parties ran in the 2011–2012 elections.

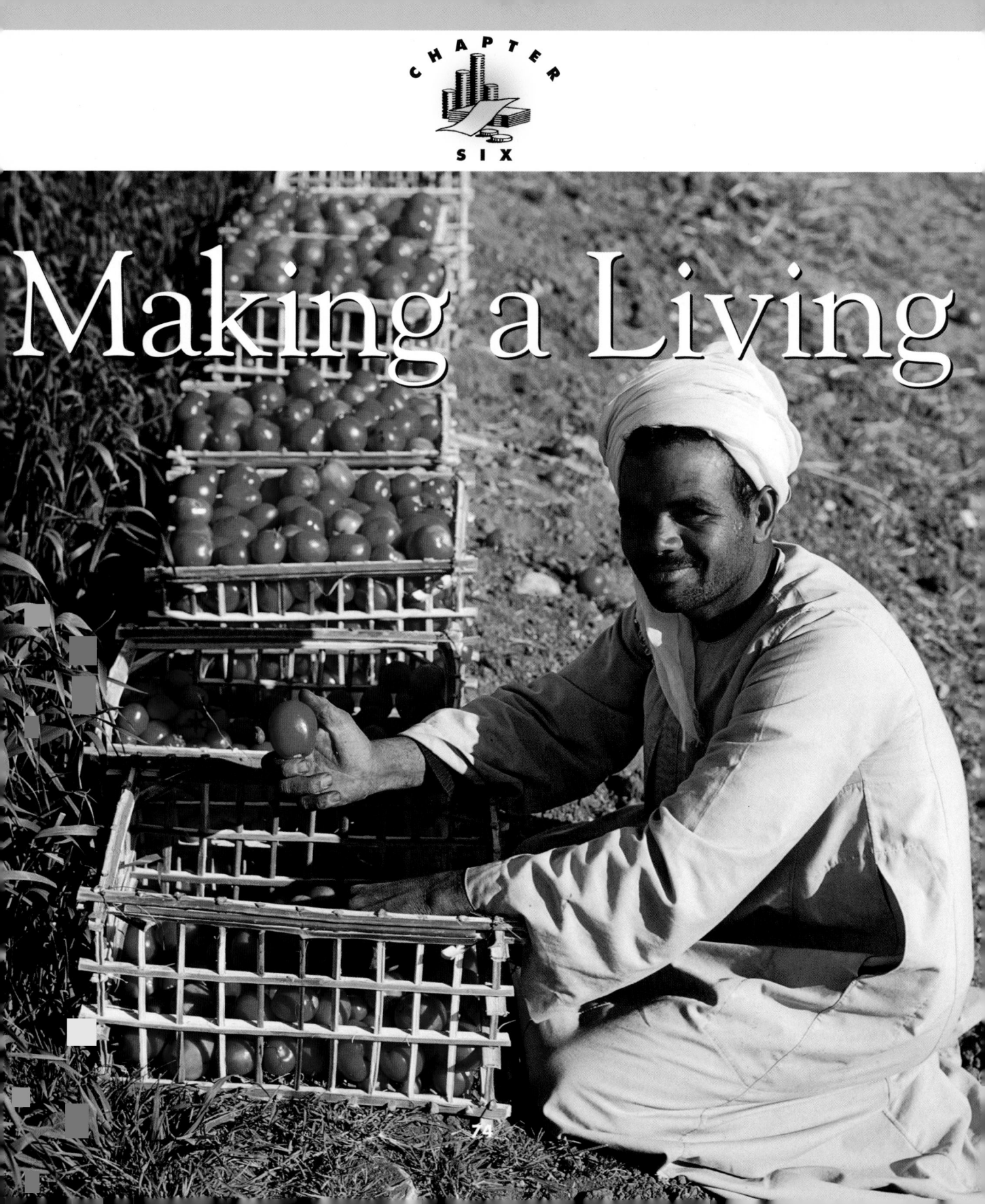

Making a Living

UNEMPLOYMENT, LOW WAGES, HIGH FOOD PRICES—these were some of the loudest complaints among protesters in Egypt's 2011 revolution.

Opposite: **A farmer harvests tomatoes near Cairo. Egypt is the fifth-largest tomato producer in the world.**

Economically, Egypt is considered a developing country. But among developing nations, Egypt's economic conditions are above average. This is partly due to economic reforms begun in the 1990s. They included irrigating the Western Desert, building new cities, developing the Mediterranean coastal strip, and building an underground transit system.

One major reform program, however, did not work out so well. That was privatization—selling government-owned industries to private companies. In the early 1990s, Egypt began selling power plants, roads, airports, banks, hotels, and many other businesses. The program eventually failed. Thousands of workers staged protests in 2010 because of lost jobs and low wages. Protesters were also angry about government officials taking payoffs for selling businesses. In response, the government canceled its privatization program.

About 30 percent of Egyptians go to college, but many have trouble finding a job.

Lack of jobs remains an urgent problem. Egypt's unemployment rate rose to almost 12 percent in the first quarter of 2011. The rate is even higher among young people in their teens and early twenties. Those with a college education are many times more likely to be unemployed than young people with only an elementary education. International agencies estimate that Egypt needs to add almost ten million more jobs to solve its employment problems.

Services

Services make up the largest sector of Egypt's economy. Service workers include teachers, medical workers, and repair people. Egypt's major service industry is tourism. Tourists pour into Egypt to see the Great Pyramid and the Sphinx. Around Luxor, they marvel at the Valley of the Kings and the temples of Karnak and Thebes. Near Aswan, they visit the temples of Philae and Ramses II.

Cruises in "floating hotels" are popular, too. These luxurious boats take visitors up the Nile, stopping at ancient sites along the way. Tourist villages operate along the Red Sea coasts at Hurghada and in the Sinai. All the tour guides, tourist shopkeepers, and tourist hotel workers are part of Egypt's tourist industry.

Money Facts

The Egyptian pound (£E) is Egypt's basic unit of currency. One pound is divided into 100 piastres. Paper money comes in values of 25 and 50 piastres and £E 1, 5, 10, 20, 50, 100, and 200. The larger the bill, the larger its value. Coins come in values of 5, 10, 20, 25, and 50 piastres and £E 1. The smaller-valued coins are rarely used. In 2011, £E 5.97 was equal to US$1, and £E 1 was equal to US$0.17.

Egyptian bills are printed in Arabic on one side and English on the other. The Arabic side features famous mosques or symbols. The English side shows antiquities such as the Sphinx, the Abu Simbel temple, the mask of Tutankhamen, and statues of Ramses II.

Weavers copy a pattern into a carpet. Textiles are an important manufactured good in Egypt.

In the 1990s, terrorist groups began attacking tourists. Other attacks occurred in the 2000s. This was a blow for Egypt's tourism industry. The 2011 revolution scared off tourists as well. Despite these incidents, tourism recovered and continues to grow.

Economic Activities as Share of GDP* (2008/2009)

Services	48.7%
Manufacturing	16.6%
Mining	14.9%
Agriculture	13.7%
Construction	4.4%
Other	1.7%

*The gross domestic product (GDP) is the total value of all goods and services a country produces in a year.

Manufacturing

Egypt's leading manufactured goods are food products, petroleum (oil) products, metal products, and cotton textiles. Textile plants spin cotton fibers into thread and yarn, weave cotton into cloth, and make finished clothing. Cotton goods are Egypt's major exports after petroleum products.

Some of Egypt's food products are processed meat and milk, canned vegetables, flour, juices, and cooking oils. Other manufactured goods include cements, chemicals, fertilizers, medicines, and steel.

In the past, the government built and owned most factories. This system is gradually changing. More and more factories are jointly owned by the government and private companies.

Mining

Thousands of years ago, Egypt's pharaohs used mining to increase their wealth. Gold, turquoise, and granite are among the treasures in Egypt's quarries and mines.

Today, oil and natural gas are Egypt's richest mineral resources. In 2011, Egypt was producing about 660,000 barrels of oil a day. Most of Egypt's oil exports go to India, with smaller amounts going to Italy and the United States. Egypt's natural gas industry is growing fast, with most of the supply coming from the Mediterranean and the Nile delta. Egypt exports much of its gas through the Arab Gas Pipeline. It carries natural gas from Egypt to Jordan, Lebanon, and Syria.

Huge offshore oil rigs operate in the Gulf of Suez, Egypt's major oil-producing region. The Nile delta and the Western Desert also have large oil and natural gas deposits. More oil and gas has been found in the Eastern

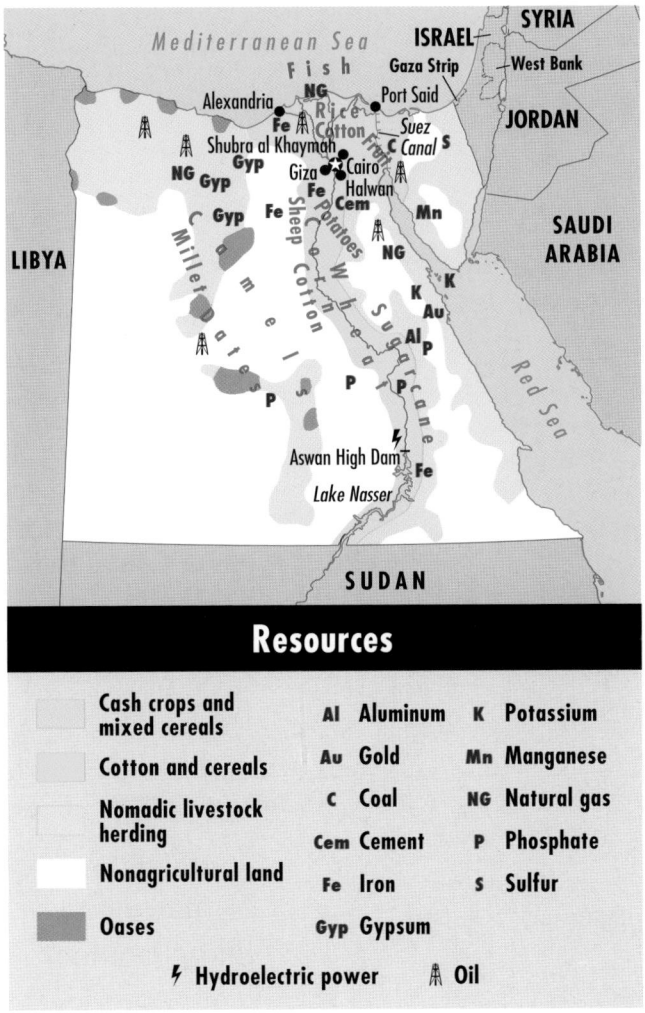

Desert and the Mediterranean. Other important minerals include iron ore, phosphates, manganese, uranium, and coal.

Agriculture

Almost one-third of Egyptian workers make their living by farming. Many are small-scale farmers along the banks of the Nile. They work the land by hand because their farms are too small for large machines.

What Egypt Grows, Makes, and Mines

Agriculture (2009)

Sugarcane	17,000,000 metric tons
Wheat	8,523,000 metric tons
Rice	7,500,000 metric tons

Manufacturing (2009, value in Egyptian pounds)

Petroleum products	£E 64,738 million
Food products	£E 44,981 million
Basic metals	£E 42,753 million

Mining (2007)

Petroleum	34.1 million metric tons
Natural gas	55,700 million cubic meters
Phosphate rock	2.2 million metric tons

Egyptian farmers bring alfalfa and livestock to market.

Crops can grow on only about 4 percent of Egypt's land. But water and year-round warm weather make the farms highly productive. Most of the farmland is in the Nile delta and the Nile River valley. Some desert regions are being developed for farming. Other farmland is disappearing as urban areas grow.

Egypt is one of the world's top producers of long-staple (long-fibered) cotton, its principal crop. The most important food crops are grains such as rice, barley, wheat, and corn. Other important crops are potatoes, onions, beans, tomatoes, and oranges. Sugarcane and dates grow year-round.

Egypt is among the world's top producers of both figs and dates. In some fields, date palms are used as shade for other crops, such as cabbage. After the dates are harvested, they are spread out on the ground to dry.

Irrigating the Land

In ancient times, Egypt had two growing seasons. Now, thanks to the Aswan High Dam, farmers are able to plant three seasons of crops. The summer season—from May to October—is the time for cotton, tomatoes, corn, rice, and potatoes. October through April is the time for growing wheat, barley, beans, onions, and berseem—a clover for animal feed. The Nile used to flood from July through October, but since the dam was built, that time is used as an extra growing season.

Pumping stations pump Nile water into wide irrigation canals along the bank. Smaller canals branch off from the main channel. Every three weeks, the canal gates are opened to flood the fields.

Irrigating the New Valley has been a dream since ancient times. Now gigantic irrigation projects are under way in the Western Desert. They involve building canals from the Nile to farming villages in the desert. Other projects involve channeling water from Lake Nasser and digging wells to reach underground water. These projects have added millions of acres to Egypt's farmable land.

Traveling by Land

Only about 3 percent of Egyptians own cars, although this may be hard to believe when you are driving in Cairo. City streets are thick with traffic. People also travel on buses, taxis, motorcycles, bicycles, and donkey carts.

With more than 31,000 miles (50,000 km) of paved roads, travel throughout Egypt is easy. Signposts are in Arabic and English, and distances are shown in kilometers. Roadways cover the Nile valley and delta. Others run along the Mediterranean and Red Sea coasts, out to the Western Desert oases, and through the Sinai. A major highway connects Cairo and Alexandria, while another runs alongside the Nile from Cairo to Aswan. A loop highway circles around the New Valley oases.

To cross the Suez Canal, motorists drive through the Ahmad Hamdi Tunnel beneath it. But travelers must be sure to plan ahead. Traffic leading to the tunnel can be heavy, and the tunnel closes at night.

Egypt's main railway line runs from Alexandria to Aswan—almost the entire length of the country. From Cairo's Ramses Station, fast passenger trains take about three hours to Alexandria and fourteen hours to Aswan.

Cairo's Metro, which opened in 1987, was Africa's first underground railway system. It has several stations in central Cairo and others in outlying areas.

About two million people ride the Cairo Metro every day.

Water and Air Travel

Egyptians travel and transport goods on the Nile, just as their ancestors did for thousands of years. Besides the river system, there are hundreds of miles of canals. Passenger ferries sail between Egyptian ports and Italy, Greece, Cyprus, and Jordan.

For international trade, ships use the Mediterranean Sea, the Red Sea, and—connecting them—the Suez Canal. The canal is just over 100 miles (160 km) long. More than twenty thousand ships pass through the Suez Canal every year. Egypt gets a great deal of income from shipping through the Suez Canal, because

A large containership travels down the Suez Canal past the city of Suez.

The Cairo International Airport is the second-busiest airport in Africa.

ships pay a fee to pass through. Alexandria, on the Mediterranean, is the nation's major port. Others are Port Said and Damietta on the Mediterranean, and Suez and Safaga on the Red Sea.

Most of the world's major airlines fly into Cairo's international airport at Heliopolis. Alexandria, Hurghada, Luxor, and Sharm el-Sheikh have international airports, too.

Communications

How did people get the word to show up in Tahrir Square for the 2011 revolution? They heard about it on the Internet, mainly through the social networking sites Facebook and Twitter. It began with Wael Ghonim, a Google executive, and

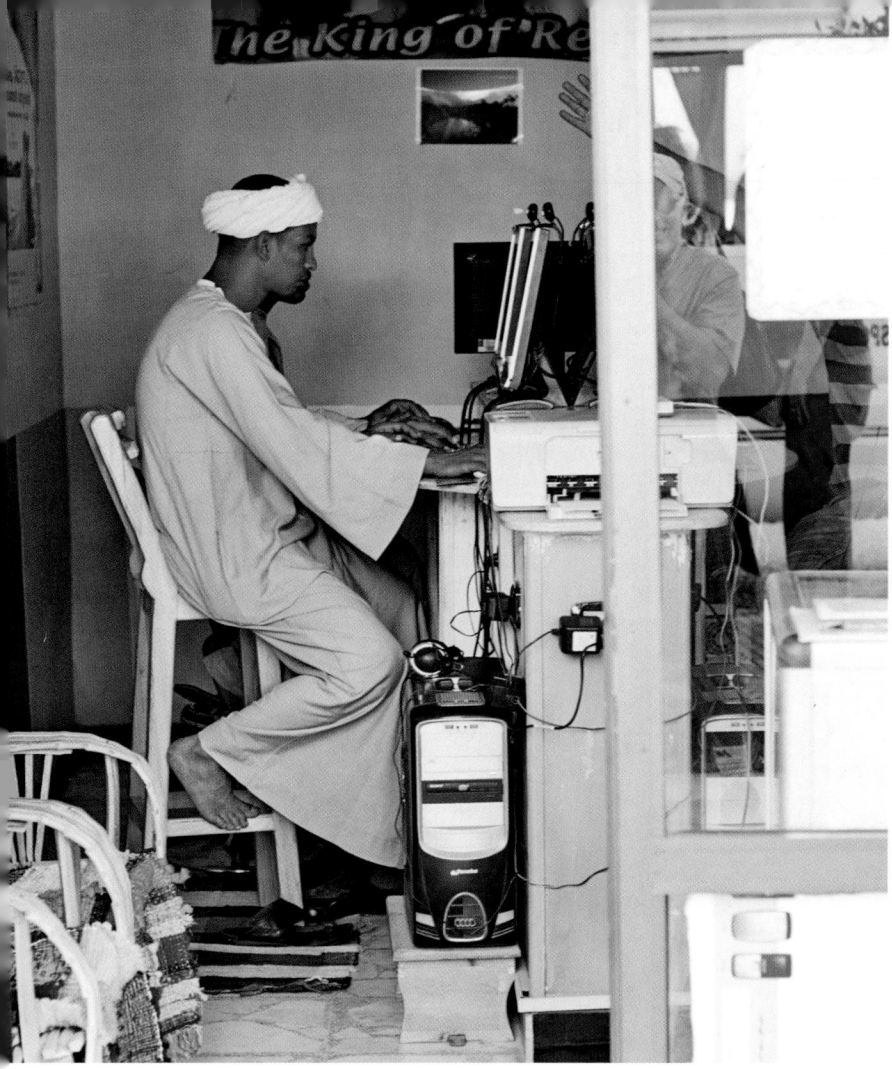

Young Egyptians used computers to plan and communicate during the 2011 revolution.

Asmaa Mahfouz, a young woman activist. They posted videos, challenges, and directions urging thousands of Egyptians to turn out for the protest. As the protest continued, more participants added posts and tweets to let others know what was going on. One young woman explained how the protesters used digital media: "We use Facebook to schedule the protests, Twitter to coordinate, and YouTube to tell the world."

Internet use is widespread, with more than twenty million Egyptians sending and receiving information online. Cell phones are everywhere. It's not unusual to see a camel driver in the desert pull out a cell phone! In 2008, more than forty-one million Egyptians had mobile phones, while there were only about twelve million landlines.

Free speech and freedom of the press are hot issues in Egypt. Under Mubarak, people who criticized the government were arrested, beaten, and imprisoned. They included bloggers, reporters, and newspaper editors. During the 2011 revolution, Internet service was shut down for days and several editors were jailed. Even the Cairo bureau of the Arabic news network Al Jazeera was closed down. Egyptians hope their new government will eliminate all censorship.

Most of Egypt's publishing and broadcasting is centered in Cairo. Of the nation's thirteen daily newspapers, the most widely read are *Al-Ahram* (*The Pyramids*), *Al-Jumhuriyah* (*The Republic*), and *Al-Akhbar* (*The News*). The *Egyptian Gazette* and *Daily News Egypt* are English-language papers. All newspapers are government supervised, and the Egyptian Radio and Television Union (ERTU) controls radio and television service. There are programs in Arabic, English, and French, and foreign broadcasts in more than thirty languages. Satellites beam Egyptian programs to the rest of the Arab world, as well as to Great Britain and the United States.

A shopkeeper in Aswan reads a newspaper.

CHAPTER SEVEN

Crowded Cities, Common Bonds

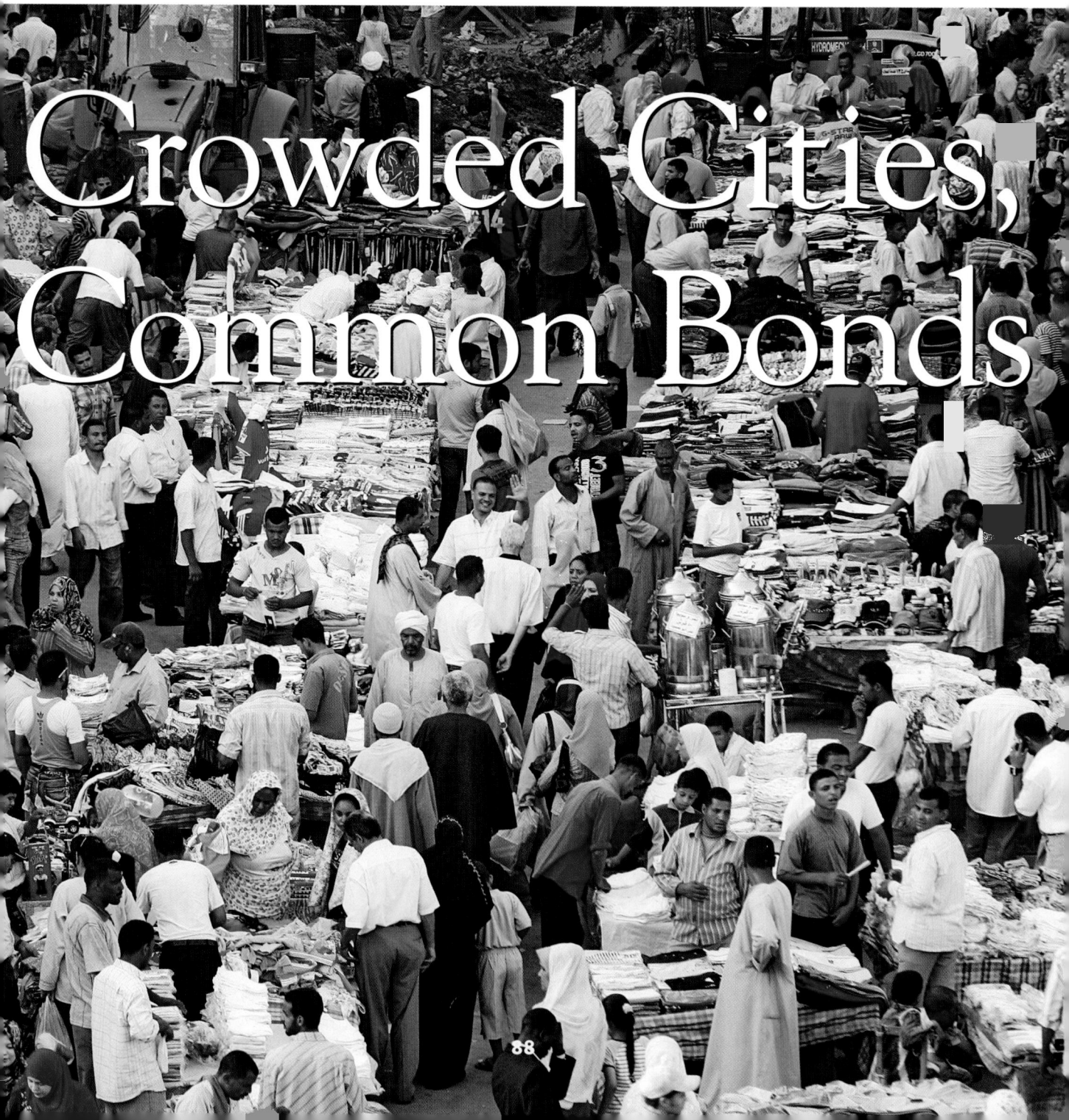

EGYPT HAS THE THIRD-HIGHEST POPULATION OF all African nations, after Nigeria and Ethiopia. In 2011, Egypt's population was estimated at about 82 million. About 99 percent of Egypt's people live in the Nile delta, along the Nile, or beside the Suez Canal. These areas are among the most densely populated in the world. Cairo and Alexandria are the largest cities. More than 18 million people live in the Cairo metropolitan area. Other densely populated cities are Giza and Port Said.

Opposite: **People pack a shopping district in Cairo.**

Small communities are clustered around the oases and irrigated desert regions. The government is trying to attract more settlers to these areas. At the same time, rural people keep moving to the cities for jobs and a better standard of living. There is a saying that every minute in Cairo, one person is born and two arrive by train.

The Sinai Peninsula is lightly populated. Many of its residents live along the Mediterranean and Red Sea coasts. Nomadic Bedouins live in the interior. They travel by camel and graze their goats and sheep on the scrubby vegetation.

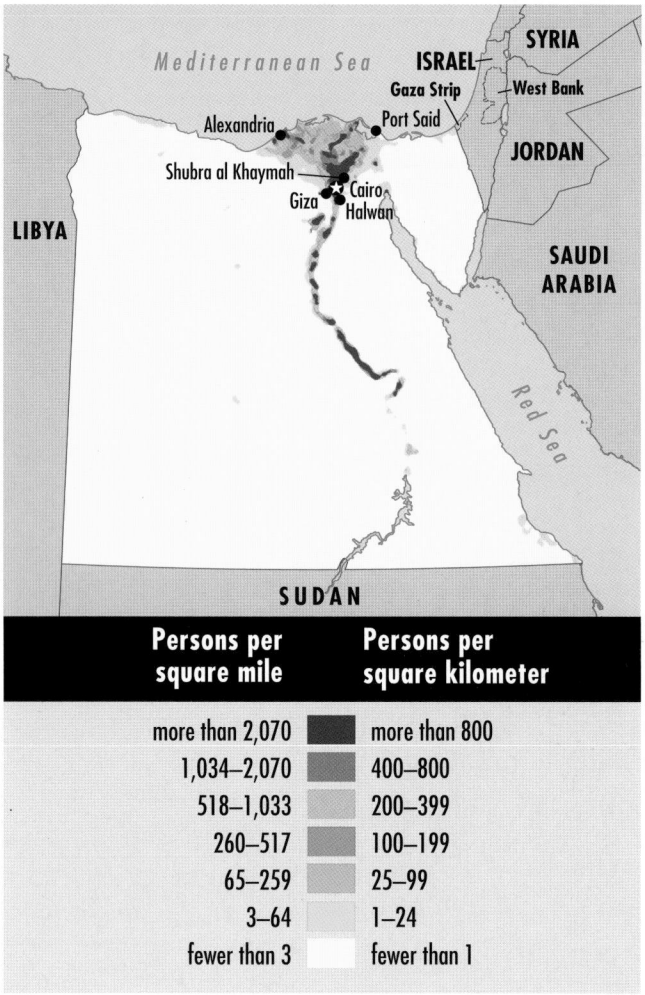

Population Growth

Egypt's population grows by more than 1.8 million people every year. This growth adds to Egypt's problems of poverty, unemployment, housing shortages, and poor nutrition.

Feeding all the people is a major problem in overpopulated Egypt. Experts say that more farmland is now used to grow food for animals than for people because of a change in Egyptians' eating habits. Beef and chicken have become increasingly popular among middle- and upper-class Egyptians, so feed must be grown for those animals.

The Youth Bubble

On average, an Egyptian can expect to live to age seventy-three. At the same time, a very large portion of the population is young. The median age in Egypt is twenty-four. That's the age that divides the population in half, with half of the people younger and half older. In contrast, the median age in the United States is thirty-seven, and Canada's median age is forty-one.

Egypt's large youth population is called the youth bubble. The bubble was a major factor in the 2011 revolution. Millions of young people were out of work, especially in Cairo, where college-educated youth expect to find good jobs. Frustrated with their employment prospects, they took to the streets to protest the government's economic policies.

Who Are the Egyptians?

Egyptians generally think of themselves as Arabs, but there is no single Egyptian "type." Over the centuries, native Egyptians mixed with a variety of people—Arabs, Berbers, Ethiopians, Persians, Turks, central Asians, Greeks, and Romans. In the south, some have blended with the Nubians of northern Sudan.

People who live in rural villages along the Nile are called *fellahin*. Many raise crops using the ancient methods and tools of their ancestors. The standard of living among the fellahin is low. Their average monthly income is less than US$50.

Population of Largest Cities (2006 est.)

Cairo	6,758,581
Alexandria	4,110,015
Giza	2,681,863
Shubra al Khaymah	1,016,722
Halwan	643,327
Port Said	570,768
Suez	510,935

Small villages dot the Nile.

Who Lives in Egypt?

Arabs (including Bedouins)	99%
Nubians and others	1%

Minority groups in Egypt include Copts, Bedouins, and Nubians. Among the many foreign nationals living in Egypt are Britons, Greeks, and Italians.

Bedouins form a small minority of Egypt's population. They are traditionally a nomadic people, although many have settled down to a farming lifestyle. Bedouins were the original people of the Sinai, and most Sinai residents today are Bedouins. Others live in the Western and Eastern Deserts. Bedouins live throughout the Middle East—not only in Egypt, but also in Saudi Arabia, Jordan, and Israel. They think of themselves as Bedouins and Arabs, rather than as citizens of one particular country.

Traditionally, Bedouins were nomads who moved from place to place, herding animals. Today, many are settled in one place.

Nubian women in Aswan

Nubians are dark-skinned, non-Arab people. Pharaohs of the Twenty-fifth Dynasty were Nubian kings. Traditionally, Nubians lived along the Nile south of Aswan and in northern Sudan. Many lost their homes when the Aswan High Dam was built. Some moved north, while others stayed in the Lake Nasser area.

Copts are a religious minority rather than an ethnic minority. They are descendants of Egyptians who lived in the days of the pharaohs. At the time of the Arab conquest, Copts formed the Christian majority. Over time, many converted from the Coptic Church to Islam. Today, some Copts are well-educated professionals, while others are very poor.

The Arabic Alphabet

a	ا	d*	ض
b	ب	t*	ط
t	ت	z*	ظ
th	ث	a pause	ع
g	ج	gh	غ
h	ح	f	ف
kh	خ	q	ق
d	د	k	ك
dh	ذ	l	ل
r	ر	m	م
z	ز	n	ن
s	س	h	ه
sh	ش	w	و
s*	ص	y	ي

*Harder sounds

Common Arabic Words and Phrases

aywa (EYE-wah)	yes
la	no
assalaamu aleikum (ah-sah-LA-moo ah-LAY-koom)	hello
ma'a salaama (MAH-ah sah-LAH-mah)	good-bye
minfadlik (min-FAHD-lik)	please (to a woman)
minfadlak (min-FAHD-lahk)	please (to a man)
shukran (shoo-KRAHN)	thank you
la shukran (LA shoo-KRAHN)	no, thank you
Feyn ... ? (FAYN)	Where is ... ?
Bekaam? (beh-KAHM)	How much?

Arabic Language and Writing

Arabic is Egypt's official language, but many Egyptians also speak English or French. The Arabic language has several forms. Classical Arabic is a complex language used in fine literature. Modern standard Arabic, which includes many new words taken from other cultures, is used in business and other official communications. At home or on the streets, people use local dialects. These can be very different from one region to another.

Arabic script is based on the alphabet of an ancient people called the Nabataeans. It is written from right to left. Arabic writings can be so decorative that they are sometimes used as art. The modern Arabic alphabet has twenty-eight characters, all consonants. Vowel sounds for a, i, and u are indicated by signs above or below a character. The digits used in the Western world—called Arabic numerals—are derived from Arabic numbers.

Coptic Language and Writing

The Coptic language grew out of the ancient Egyptian language. The Coptic form of the language began to emerge in the 100s CE. By the time of the Arab invasion, Coptic was Egypt's everyday language. Then, for many years, both Arabic and Coptic were commonly spoken. But by the 1600s, spoken Coptic survived only in remote villages. The language is preserved today in Coptic Christian religious services. Today, only a few hundred native Coptic speakers survive.

Coptic writing had a history of its own. Ancient hieroglyphic writing changed into a script called demotic. When the Ptolemies came to power, Egyptians began writing the Coptic

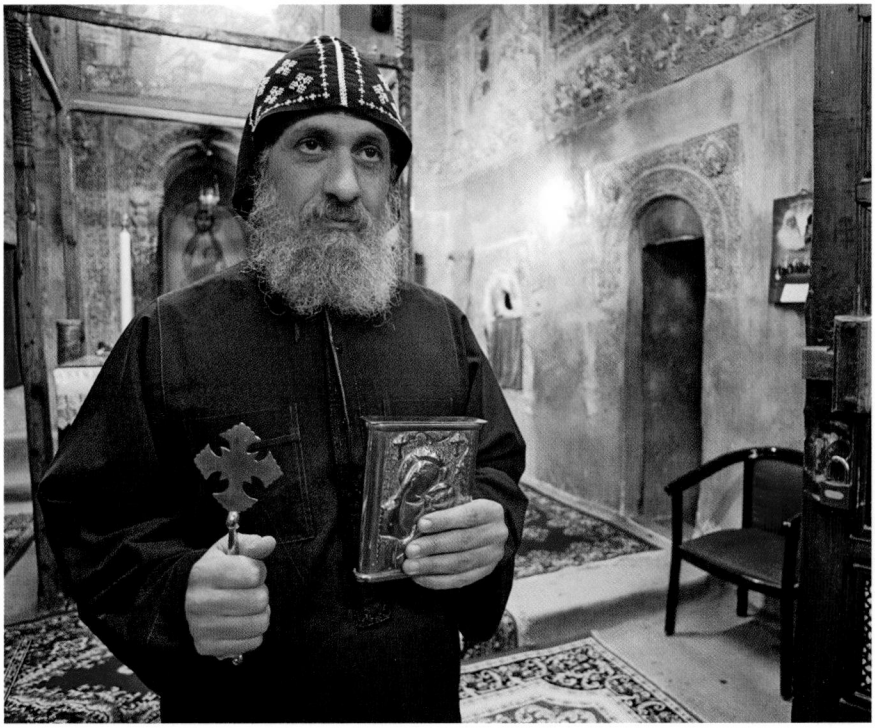

Copts make up an estimated 9 percent of the Egyptian population.

language with the Greek alphabet, adding seven demotic letters. In the 300s CE, Copts translated the Bible from Greek into Coptic, and written Coptic took its final form. Coptic monks continue to preserve the script in prayer books.

Education

Egypt offers free public education from primary school through the university level. By law, children must attend school from ages six through fourteen. Primary school covers the first six grades. Next comes three years of preparatory school. Students who finish this level have completed their schooling requirements. But about one-fourth of students drop out after primary

Some Egyptian children wear uniforms to school, while others follow a school's modest dress code.

school. Many need to work to help support their families. Students who complete preparatory school can continue on for three years of secondary school.

About 66 percent of Egypt's adults can read and write. That includes about 75 percent of Egyptian men and 58 percent of Egyptian women. Hoping to correct the gender divide, the government has set up programs to encourage girls to get an education. Many more girls are going to school now and staying until they graduate.

About 52 percent of the students at Cairo University are women.

Graduates of Egyptian universities are well prepared for professional life. The nation has about two dozen public universities, about thirty private universities, and dozens of technical institutes and teachers' colleges. More than two hundred thousand students are enrolled in Cairo University. Alexandria University is another important institution. Egypt's oldest university is the one-thousand-year-old Al-Azhar University in Cairo. It is a major center of learning for the Islamic world.

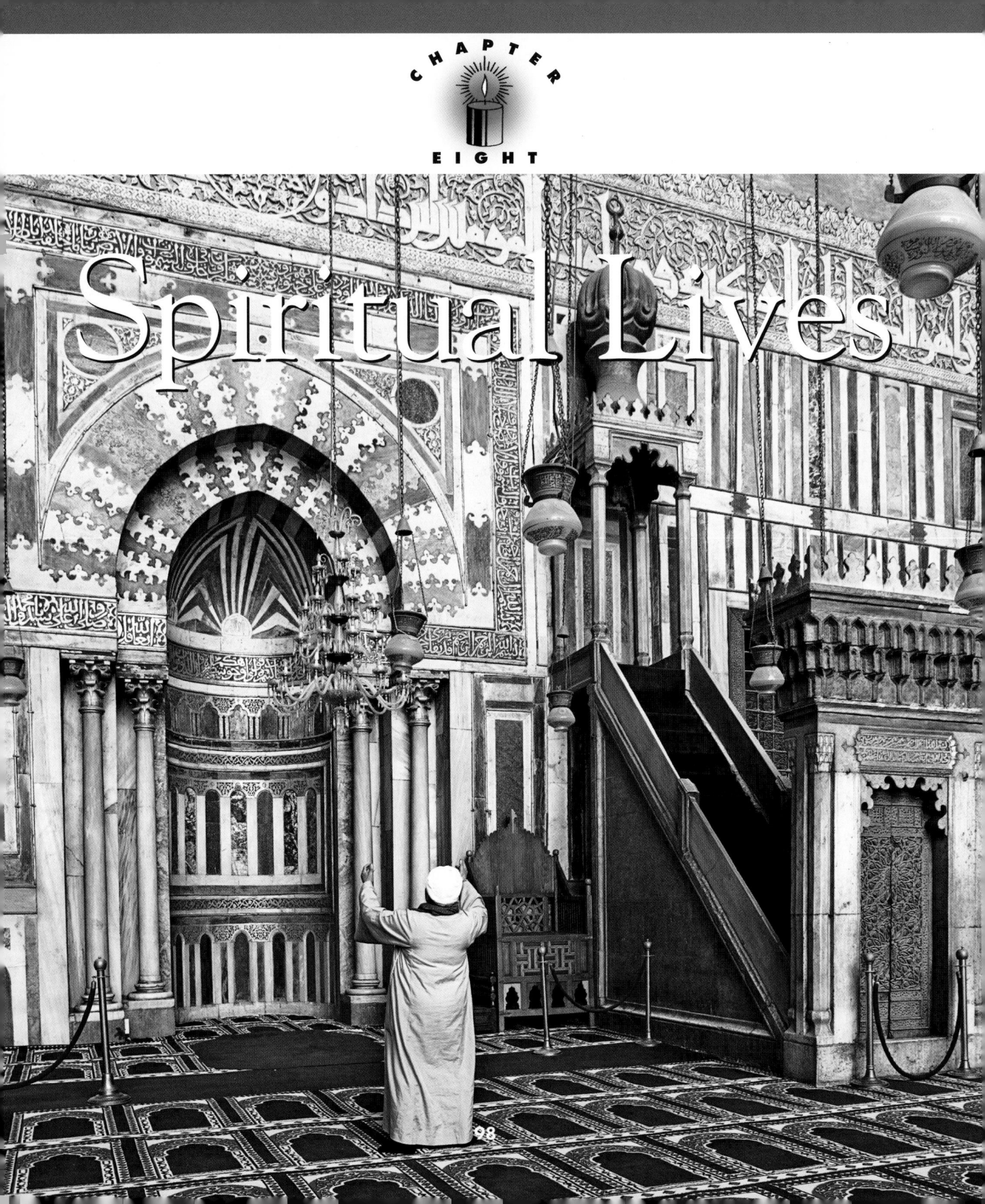

CHAPTER EIGHT

Spiritual Lives

ISLAM IS EGYPT'S OFFICIAL RELIGION, AND THE MAJORITY of Egyptians are Muslims. Most Egyptian Muslims belong to the Sunni branch of Islam, while a small minority belong to the Shi'i sect. According to the constitution, people of all religions are free to practice their faith. At times, however, non-Muslims and even Shi'is have been targets of persecution.

Islam, which means "submission," is the religion of the entire Arab world. Its followers are Muslim, meaning "one who submits." Islam is monotheistic, meaning it holds a belief in only one god. *Allah* is the word for "God" in Arabic.

The Prophet Muhammad was the person who first preached about Islam. Muslims believe that God revealed his teachings to Muhammad through the angel Gabriel. These revelations are written down in the Qur'an, Islam's holy book. Islamic teachings cover every aspect of daily life—food, clothing, education, and manners.

Opposite: **The Sultan Hassan Mosque, which was completed in about 1362, is one of the most beautiful mosques in Cairo.**

Shoes are left at the entrance to a mosque in Bahariya.

When Muslims worship in mosques, they leave their shoes at the door. The muezzin calls the faithful to prayer from the minaret, the mosque's tower. Five times a day, wherever they are, devout Muslims kneel to pray, facing the holy city of Mecca in Saudi Arabia. In most Islamic cities today, loudspeakers broadcast the call to prayer.

All faithful Muslims practice the Five Pillars of Faith: (1) believing in one God and that Muhammad is his messenger; (2) praying five times a day, facing the holy city of Mecca; (3) giving aid to the needy; (4) fasting during the month of Ramadan; and (5) making a pilgrimage (hajj) to Mecca at least once in their lives.

Egypt's Religions

Muslim	90%
Coptic Christian	9%
Other	1%

The Islamic Calendar

Muslims divide the year into twelve months of twenty-nine or thirty days each, following the cycles of the moon. The Islamic year is 354 days long (355 in leap years)—eleven days shorter than a year in the Western calendar. So each year, feast days fall eleven days earlier than the year before. Year zero in the Islamic calendar is 622 CE, the year of the hegira, Muhammad's flight to Medina to avoid persecution.

Ramadan and Other Festivals

The month of Ramadan is Egypt's most festive season. During Ramadan, Muslims celebrate Muhammad's receiving the Qur'an from God. All month, they fast, taking neither food nor water from sunup to sundown. In Cairo, a cannon fires from the Citadel of Saladin at sunset, announcing that it is time for *iftar*, the feast that breaks the fast.

The Prophet

Born around 570 CE, Muhammad was a merchant in the Arabian city of Mecca. At the time, the scattered tribes of Arabia had a variety of local gods. According to tradition, one day the angel Gabriel appeared to Muhammad in the desert. He told Muhammad to teach people to worship the one and only God. Merchants in Mecca were angered at Muhammad's teachings. In 622, they drove him out, and he fled to the city of Medina. His flight, called the hegira, is marked as the beginning of Islam.

Major Muslim Holidays

	2012	2013
Moulid an-Nabi (Muhammad's birthday)	February 4	January 24
Beginning of Ramadan	July 20	July 9
'Id al-Fitr (end of Ramadan)	August 19	August 8
'Id al-Adha (Feast of the Sacrifice)	October 26	October 15
Ras al-Sana al-Hegira (Islamic New Year)	November 15	November 4

A traditional iftar begins with dates and apricots. Next comes lentil soup, meat pies, vegetables, and pastries. Feasting and parties go on through the night. Strings of lights and lanterns (*fanus*) brighten the streets, and boys shoot off firecrackers. At sunrise, the fasting begins again. Ramadan is also a time for exchanging good wishes and being especially generous to the poor. The feast of 'Id al-Fitr marks the end of Ramadan.

A man buys his daughter a tin lantern. These lanterns are traditional during Ramadan.

Families begin the celebration of 'Id al-Adha with prayers.

Other important festivals are Ras al-Sana al-Hegira (Islamic New Year) and 'Id al-Adha (Feast of the Sacrifice). Some holidays are *moulids*—festivals honoring a holy person. Moulid an-Nabi is Muhammad's birthday. In Cairo, a fantastic procession surges through the streets, and the night is ablaze with lights. Each town also celebrates the moulid of its own patron saint.

Coptic Christians

Coptic Christians form the largest religious minority in Egypt. They are the remnant of Egypt's Christian community before the Arab conquest. The church's official name is the Coptic

A monk enters a Coptic church in Hurghada, in the Sinai.

Orthodox Church of Alexandria. It is difficult to say how many Coptic Christians live in Egypt today. The Egyptian government estimates the number of Copts at 6 to 10 percent of the population. Other sources place estimates at 15 percent.

Copts enjoy freedom of worship in Egypt but may not preach their religion to others. While Copts may convert to Islam, Muslims may not convert to the Coptic Church. In some areas, Copts have been targets of brutal attacks by Muslim extremists.

Saint Mark is believed to have brought Christianity to Egypt in the first century CE. The new faith blended well with Egyptians' ancient beliefs, such as the final judgment and the importance of the afterlife. Christianity's first monasteries were set up in the deserts of Egypt. The first Christian monk, Saint Anthony, was a Copt.

Easter and the season of Lent before Easter are the most important times in the religious calendar. During Lent, priests and monks fast from sunrise to sunset. Even after sunset, they have no meat, fish, eggs, wine, or coffee. The fast ends on Palm Sunday, a week before Easter. At the midnight service, the priests bless palm branches, which the people weave into crosses.

Copts have special reverence for the Holy Family—Jesus, Mary, and Joseph. Tradition holds that the Holy Family fled to Egypt to escape persecution. Coptic boys are baptized when they are forty days old, and girls are baptized at eighty days. Copts believe that the soul remains with the body for forty days after death.

Coptic clergymen bless a baby.

Pope Shenouda III has been the head of the Coptic Church since 1971.

The head of the Coptic Church—the Patriarch of Alexandria—oversees Coptic churches and monasteries throughout Egypt. The most famous historical churches are in Old Cairo on the ruins of the Roman fortress of Babylon. Several fourth-century Coptic monasteries stand at Wadi Natrun in the desert northwest of Cairo.

In 2003, Coptic Christmas was made a national holiday in Egypt. It falls on January 7 every year. Before that, Egypt's

Major Coptic Holidays

Christmas	January 7
Epiphany	January 19
Palm Sunday	One week before Easter
Easter	Date varies, depending on the spring equinox
Pentecost	Fifty days after Easter

Coptic Christians had to take it as a day off from work. This was the first time a Coptic Christian holiday was given official government recognition.

Other Religious Groups

A small minority of Egyptians belongs to other Christian groups. These include the Roman Catholic, Anglican, and Greek Orthodox churches.

A large Jewish community once flourished in Egypt. Jewish scholars translated many works of science and philosophy into Greek. They also translated the Bible's Old Testament from Hebrew into Greek. From this version, translations were made into Coptic and Latin. Today, fewer than five hundred Jewish people live in Egypt. The twelfth-century Ben Ezra Synagogue, in Old Cairo, is no longer used for worship.

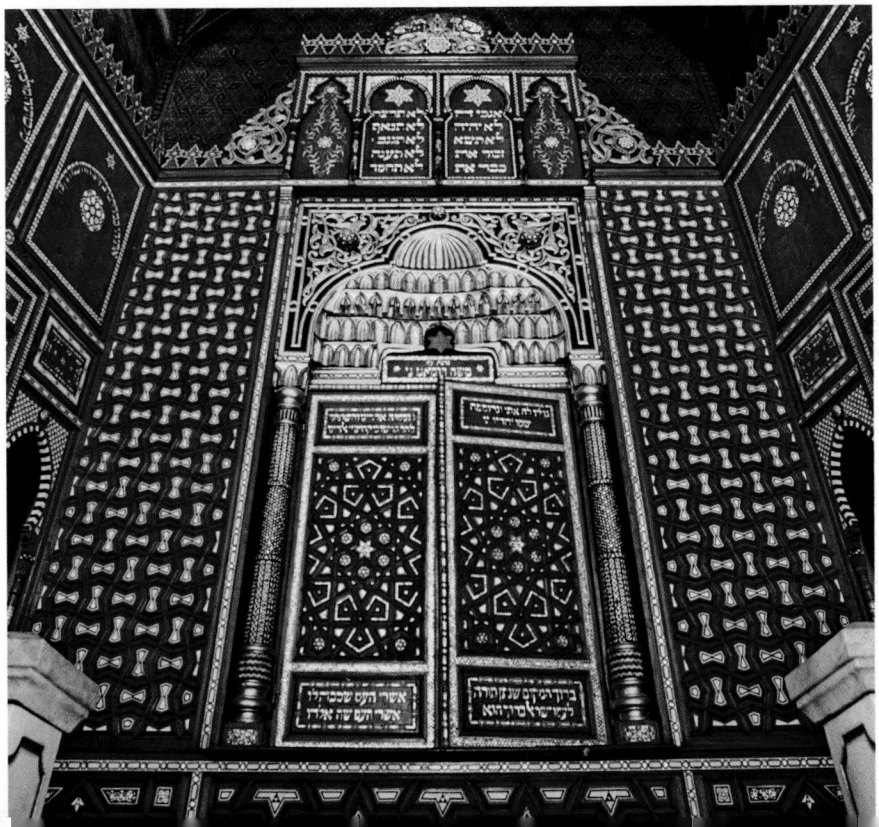

Ben Ezra Synagogue is the most visited Jewish site in Cairo.

Culture and Fun

STAND BLINDFOLDED IN THE BUSTLING STREETS OF Khan al-Khalili, and your nose will tell you where you are. Roses, cinnamon, and dozens of other sweet and savory smells fill the air. Merchants in this medieval Cairo bazaar are famous for their exotic perfumes and spices.

Opposite: **People throng Khan al-Khalili every day.**

Other craftspeople sell handblown glass, handwoven textiles, gold jewelry, and leather goods such as camel saddles. There are carved wooden boxes and trays inlaid with mother-of-pearl; brass and copper vases, cups, and trays; and statues made of alabaster, a cloudy white stone. Cotton fabric is sold here, too. Egypt's cotton cloth is known for its beautiful colors and designs.

Down the highway south of Cairo, children are busy with needles and looms. They are learning to make traditional wall hangings and carpets at the Ramses Wissa Wassef Art Centre in the village of Harrania. Their work is known around the world for its bold colors and playful designs.

Egyptian musical instruments are very much like those in the rest of the Arab world. They include the *oud* (a stringed instrument), the *rabab* (a two-stringed fiddle), and the *nay* (a flute), as well as drums and tambourines. Musicians often improvise when they perform, and audience members sometimes clap along with the rhythm.

Some of the Arab world's most popular musicians have been Egyptians. One was Sayed Darwish (1892–1923), known as the father of Egyptian popular music. He composed Egypt's national anthem. The best-loved female singer in the history of Arab music was Umm Kulthum (1898–1975). More than

An Egyptian musician plays the oud in concert. Most ouds have eleven strings.

The Cairo Opera House, which opened in 1988, is a cultural center for the city.

three million grief-stricken fans joined her funeral procession in Cairo. Umm Kulthum's nickname was Star of the East. In 2001, the Star of the East Museum opened in Cairo to celebrate her life and work.

A recent favorite is the pop star Amr Diab. He won the World Music Award for Middle Eastern music four times. Diab, who sings and plays an Egyptian style of rock, is the best-selling Arabic music artist ever.

Egyptians have many other music tastes. Some musicians are keeping alive the folk music of rural Egypt. Others compose Egyptian-style music on Western instruments. Egypt's grandest music venue is the Cairo Opera House, on Gezira Island. It presents opera, orchestra, and dance shows by Arabic artists and visiting foreign artists.

Belly dancing is popular in Egypt, as it is in much of the Middle East. While the most conservative Muslims frown on belly dancing, others see it as a fine art. In Egypt, belly dancers perform in hotels and nightclubs and at celebrations such as birthdays and weddings.

Literature and Films

Novelist Naguib Mahfouz (1911–2006), Egypt's greatest modern writer, has been called the inventor of the Arabic novel. His stories of Egyptian life earned him the 1988 Nobel Prize in Literature. That is the world's highest literary honor. Abbas al-Aqqad (1889–1964) is viewed as the greatest modern Arab poet. Even when he was imprisoned for political crimes, he continued to write deeply moving poetry.

Other Egyptian writers have also made their mark. Taha Hussein (1889–1973), minister of education from 1950 to 1952, is honored for his intellectual essays. Mahmud Taymur

The Egyptian Museum

The Egyptian Museum in Cairo highlights five thousand years of Egyptian history. It holds a collection of more than one hundred thousand artifacts, including treasures from Tutankhamen's tomb. In a special room of royal mummies, the preserved bodies of ancient pharaohs are displayed in glass cases. During the 2011 revolution, vandals broke into the museum, stealing and damaging several precious artifacts. However, the museum opened again to visitors soon after the uprising, as museum workers continued with repairs.

Naguib Mahfouz

In 1988, the novelist Naguib Mahfouz (1911–2006) became the first Arabic-language writer to win the Nobel Prize in Literature. Mahfouz is best known for his *Cairo Trilogy*, which follows the story of one family from the years of World War I to the 1950s. In 1994, Islamic extremists tried to kill Mahfouz. They were protesting his use of Muhammad as a character in his novel *Children of Gebelawi*.

(1894–1973) satirized Egyptian society in popular plays. Through essays and poems, Malak Hifni Nasif (1886–1918) tried to raise the status of Egyptian women.

Egypt's film industry is small but growing. The first Egyptian film was *The Civil Servant*, made in 1922. Since then, Egypt has produced every kind of film, from musical comedy to serious drama. Censorship, severe at times, is more relaxed now. Today, Mohamed Khan and Marwan Hamed are two of Egypt's outstanding film directors.

Mohamed Khan has made more than twenty films, including *In the Heliopolis Flat*.

Sports and Recreation

Soccer is Egypt's national sport. Kids play anywhere they can—on school teams, in side streets, or in open fields. The most popular Egyptian soccer clubs are Ahly and Zamalek. When they compete in the annual Cairo Derby, the city practically shuts down for the victory parties and parades. Egypt's national team, the Pharaohs, won the Africa Cup of Nations championship a record seven times by 2010. Squash, tennis, handball, basketball, and volleyball are popular sports, too.

Breeding, training, and racing horses have a long tradition in Egypt. During the Mameluke period, horsemanship became

Mohamed Barakat (in red) of the Egyptian Pharaohs dives for the ball during a game against Ivory Coast during the Africa Cup of Nations.

Gedo Nails It!

Mohamed "Gedo" Nagy (1984–) scored the game-winning goal against Ghana in the 2010 Africa Cup of Nations finals. The 1–0 victory was sweet. It earned the Pharaohs their seventh Africa Cup championship. Gedo was brought in only as a substitute during the tournament, but he ended up being the top scorer, with five goals overall.

Gedo's career began at age seventeen, when he joined a small soccer club in Damanhur, northwest of Cairo. Three years later, in 2005, he signed up with the Union Alexandria Sporting Club, one of Egypt's largest teams. Gedo joined the Pharaohs in 2009 and went on to score in many international tournaments.

a high art. Today, there are riding and racing clubs in Cairo, Alexandria, and other cities.

Graceful white sails float along the Mediterranean, the Red Sea, and the Nile. They are either standard sailboats or *feluccas*—Egypt's traditional flat-bottomed boats. Windsurfing, waterskiing, rowing, and fishing are some other popular water sports. Rowers from around the world compete in the Nile International Rowing Competition. Egypt also hosts national and international fishing festivals every year.

The Red Sea is one of the world's best places for scuba diving and snorkeling. Its coral reefs are spectacular. Sharm el-Sheikh, on the Sinai Peninsula, is one of the finest locations. Other good diving spots are Ras Muhammad National Park, Dahab, Hurghada, and Safaga.

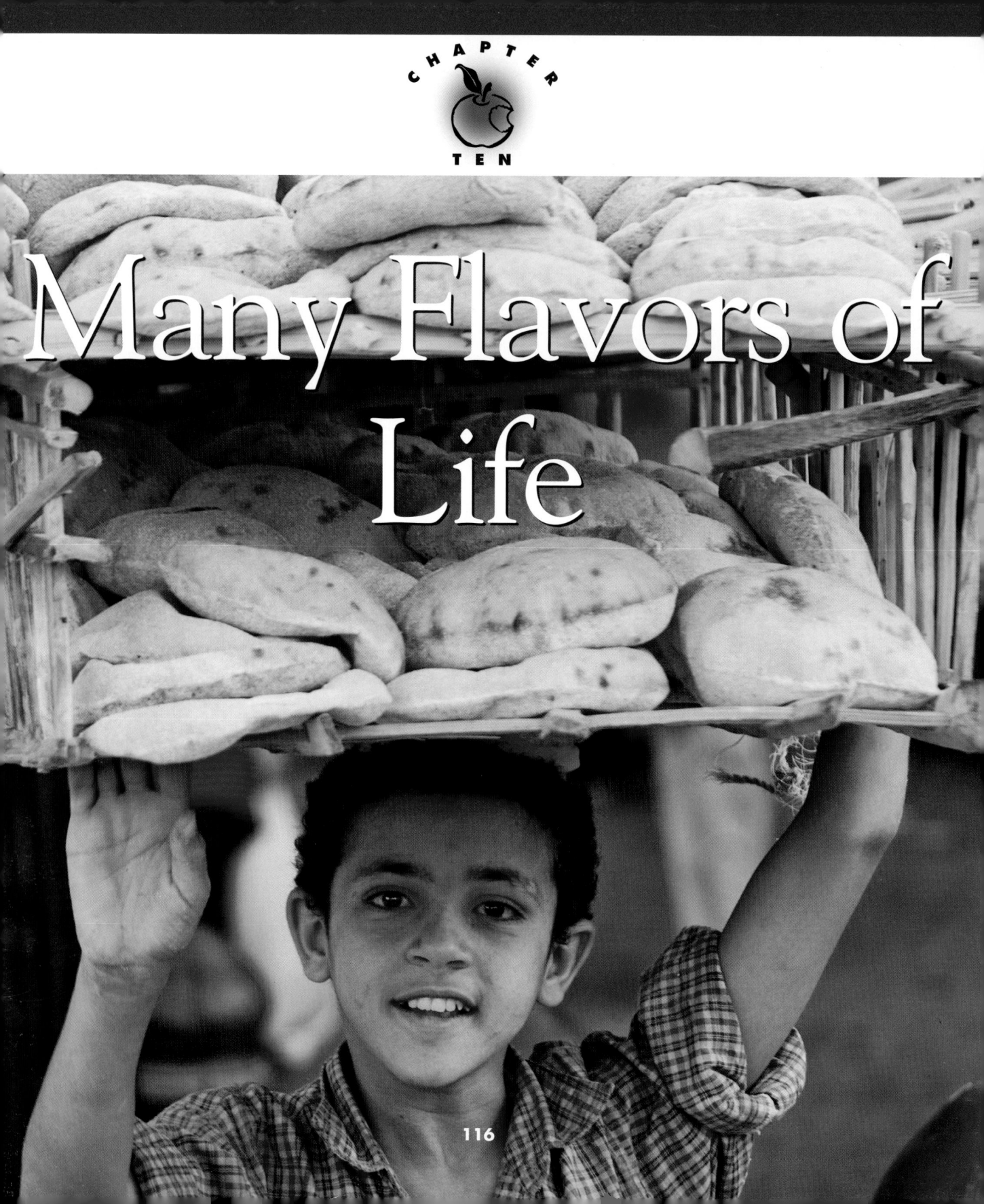

Many Flavors of Life

FOOD IS A DELIGHTFUL PART OF EGYPTIAN LIFE. FOR AN Egyptian villager, food is simple and hearty. Most meals include a dish made with fava beans. The beans are boiled for hours, often overnight, to make them soft enough to eat. Sometimes they're chopped and mixed with eggs. For a different taste, a ball or patty of soft beans can be fried in olive oil to make *tamiya*. In *ful*, the national dish, the beans are mixed with various herbs and spices for flavor.

Opposite: **A young boy sells bread in Cairo.**

Tahini is a tasty sesame-seed paste used as a dip or sandwich spread. When chickpeas, lemon juice, and garlic are added, it becomes hummus. Baba ghanoush is another dipping paste, made with eggplant and sesame. Cubes of veal or lamb are often served on skewers as kebabs. *Karkadé* is tea made with hibiscus flowers.

Aysh, Egyptian bread, is round and flat. It puffs up to make a handy pocket for meat or vegetables. Women bake bread in clay ovens, much as their ancestors did. Egyptians often use bread, instead of a spoon, to scoop up food.

Getting Your Fill of *Ful*

Egypt's national dish—*ful*—is especially popular as a breakfast food. There are as many versions of ful as there are cooks. To prepare ful, cook fava beans slowly for hours until soft. Mash garlic with sea salt and add lemon juice and olive oil. Stir this mixture in with the beans, along with chopped onions and parsley. Sprinkle with paprika and other savory spices. Serve with bread wedges, spring onions, and radishes.

Milk from cows, oxen, sheep, and goats is made into cheese. In rural areas, women fill a sheepskin or a goatskin with milk. They hang the skin up by strings and gently push it back and forth. In time, heat from the sun and acids from the skin ferment the liquid, and it forms curds, or lumps of cheese.

Egyptians drink Turkish-style coffee—thick (almost muddy), black, and strong. People can choose to take it sweet, medium, or bitter. Tea, with sugar but no milk, is another popular drink.

Traditional Clothes

To wear the veil or not to wear the veil? In Egypt, a woman's dress style is a religious issue. Islamic law requires a woman to dress modestly. For the most conservative Muslims, this means wearing the *niqab*—a long dress and veil that shows only the eyes. Many women enjoy the comfort and privacy the niqab gives them in public. At home, among family and close friends, they may wear casual clothes.

Less conservative women wear the *hijab*. It is a traditional headscarf that covers the hair but leaves the face uncovered. The hijab is popular because it honors Islamic law while making it easier to perform daily activities. Women doctors, professors, and engineers as well as students and housewives are seen wearing both styles of dress.

Many women consider themselves good Muslims, yet choose to dress in Western clothes. Some women start out wearing Western clothes when they are young, then switch to the veil when they are older.

Many Egyptian women wear headscarves with Western clothing.

Loose, light-colored clothing is traditional in Egypt. It helps people stay cool in the brutal heat.

The traditional dress for Egyptian men is the *galabiyya*—a full-length, loose-fitting robe. Villagers wear the *baladi*-style robe, with a rounded neck and wide sleeves. Saudi-style robes are buttoned up to the neck. They fit more closely, and the sleeves have cuffs. The *efrangi* style has a collar and cuffs like those on Western dress shirts. Many men wear a traditional Arabic checked scarf wrapped around the head like a turban. Some wear the typical Islamic skullcap called a *kufi*.

Housing: Bursting at the Seams

In Cairo and Alexandria, most people live in apartment buildings. Apartments

Nonreligious National Holidays

New Year's Day	January 1
National Police Day	January 25
Sham an-Nessim	March or April
Sinai Liberation Day	April 25
Labor Day	May 1
Evacuation Day	June 18
Revolution Day	July 23
Flooding of the Nile	August 15*
Armed Forces Day	October 6
Suez Day	October 24
Victory Day	December 23

*May vary by a few days

range from palatial to closet-size. Most are rented, although some may be owned by the resident. In some new apartment complexes in Cairo, apartments can cost up to several million dollars. In finer suburbs, single-family houses may have marble floors with hot-water pipes beneath the floors for warmth. But most Egyptians do not live in such nice surroundings.

There are many modern apartment buildings in Cairo.

Sniffing the Breeze

Sham an-Nessim is the day people throw open the windows and take a deep breath. This springtime "fresh air" holiday is believed to have originated in the time of the pharaohs. It falls on the Monday after Coptic Easter. Sham an-Nessim means "sniffing the breeze." Families enjoy picnics that day and eat fish, onions, and colored eggs.

Cairo does not have enough housing for its growing population. People live and sleep wherever they can—on rooftops, in garbage dumps, or on boats. Parents, grandparents, and children often live in tiny two- or three-room apartments. "If you fainted," some like to say, "you would not fall down."

Some people have even set up homes in cemeteries. A district of sultans' tombs on the east edge of Cairo is known as the City of the Dead. More than one hundred thousand people live there. Those residents have their own schools, shops, and mosques. Even some middle-class people live in the

The City of the Dead was built as an Arab cemetery in 642 CE.

A rural home in central Egypt. The thick walls block out the heat and keep the rooms cool.

City of the Dead. They find it quieter and less crowded than the city center.

Rural residents—the fellahin—live in one-story houses with flat roofs made of straw or palm wood. The thick walls are made of mud or sunbaked mud bricks. In hot weather, the roof is a cool place to sleep.

Many rural houses have dirt floors and no electricity or running water. People sit on mats or benches around a low table. Some people paint their houses with blue trim to ward off evil. Those who have made a pilgrimage to Mecca paint scenes from their trip on the outside walls.

An Ancient Game Lives On

Mancala may be the oldest board game in the world. It originated in Egypt around 1400 BCE. Today, it's a popular game for both kids and adults throughout Africa and other regions of the world. Many versions of the game exist. *Kenet, oware, woaley, bao,* and *olinda kaliya* are just a few of mancala's local names. The word *mancala* itself is Arabic for "to move" or "to transfer."

The game board is a long rectangle with two rows of six cups each—one row for each player—and a large cup on each end. The forty-eight game pieces can be pebbles, peas, or seeds. Players move their pieces from cup to cup and try to capture each other's pieces. Whoever ends up with the most pieces is the winner.

Village Life

Most fellahin are farmers. They live in small villages along the Nile, as their ancestors did thousands of years ago. Some own their land, while others rent land or work for landowners.

Villagers eat breakfast at about 6 a.m. before starting to work. Boys take the sheep and goats out to graze. When they are older, their fathers teach them traditional farming methods. Women bake bread in outdoor ovens. Girls milk goats, feed chickens, and fetch water from the village well, balancing baskets, water jars, or stacks of bread on their heads. The workday ends at sundown, and then everyone gathers for the evening meal of rice, vegetables, and ful.

City Life

A young boy sells magazines that he has fished out of a garbage bin. His father shines shoes, and his mother sells bread. Many thousands of people in Cairo are unemployed. Those who work may be executives, clerks, factory workers, shopkeepers, or street merchants. Child labor is illegal, but many children work long hours to help their families survive.

Almost half of all Egyptians live in urban areas. Villagers who can no longer survive on farms pour into the cities every day. Many bring along their goats and chickens. The first surprise they get is air pollution. Cairo's levels of dust and lead are among the highest in the world. Cairo's public buses are packed, and traffic is thick and wild. Drivers are aggressive and seem to make up their own rules.

Marriage, Egyptian Style

Some young adults in Egypt choose their own marriage partners. However, many marriages are still arranged by the parents of the bride and groom. The couple is legally married after meeting in the bride's house or a mosque and signing the official wedding contract. Next comes the public celebration. In cities, the party is held in a hotel or wedding hall. In rural areas, it takes place outdoors under a huge tent. When the two arrive, they are greeted by friends and family, along with musicians and belly dancers, in a parade called the *zaffa*. Then the pair sits on throne-like chairs for toasts, speeches, and dances. Finally, dinner is served, and guests enjoy a massive banquet.

Those who can afford it leave Cairo on weekends and in the hot summer months. Many go to Alexandria or other Mediterranean cities. There they enjoy cool sea breezes, cleaner air, less noise, and more space. Others may go to Sharm el-Sheikh and other resort towns along the Sinai Peninsula coast.

In the cities, people eat breakfast around 7:30 a.m. Lunch is in mid-afternoon, and dinner is served at 10 p.m. or later. Many shops and businesses close for a two- or three-hour mid-day break. For Muslims, Friday is the holy day of the week, and many businesses close or have shorter hours on this day.

Children play on a beach in Alexandria.

Men relax at a café in Alexandria.

Egyptian men enjoy getting together in cafés to drink Turkish coffee, play backgammon, and smoke water pipes. People from all walks of life like to relax in outdoor cafés where they can sit back and watch the vibrant life of the city around them.

Sidewalk vendors sell live chickens, papyrus paintings, and sweets. Cars and bicycles swerve around long-robed men guiding donkey carts. Women scurry through the maze, balancing jars or platters on their heads. Even in narrow alleys, people seem to follow unspoken "rules of the road." They know that if they give an inch here and there, everyone gets what they need.

Timeline

Egyptian History

King Menes founds the kingdom of Egypt by unifying Upper and Lower Egypt.	**ca. 3100** BCE
Pharaoh Khufu builds the Great Pyramid of Giza.	**ca. 2500** BCE
The New Kingdom begins, with Thebes as the capital of Egypt.	**1539** BCE
King Tutankhamen dies at about age eighteen.	**1352** BCE
The Persians conquer Egypt.	**525** BCE
Alexander the Great takes over Egypt and builds Alexandria as his capital.	**332** BCE
Egypt becomes part of the Roman Empire.	**30** BCE
Muslim Arab armies conquer Egypt.	**642** CE
The Fatimid dynasty begins its rule over Egypt.	**969**
Saladin establishes the Ayyubid dynasty.	**1171**
The Mamelukes take control of Egypt.	**1250**
Ottoman Turks invade Egypt and rule for almost three hundred years.	**1517**

World History

ca. 2500 BCE	Egyptians build the pyramids and the Sphinx in Giza.
ca. 563 BCE	The Buddha is born in India.
313 CE	The Roman emperor Constantine legalizes Christianity.
610	The Prophet Muhammad begins preaching a new religion called Islam.
1054	The Eastern (Orthodox) and Western (Roman Catholic) Churches break apart.
1095	The Crusades begin.
1215	King John seals the Magna Carta.
1300s	The Renaissance begins in Italy.
1347	The plague sweeps through Europe.
1453	Ottoman Turks capture Constantinople, conquering the Byzantine Empire.
1492	Columbus arrives in North America.
1500s	Reformers break away from the Catholic Church, and Protestantism is born.

Egyptian History

Napoléon Bonaparte invades Egypt.	**1798**
The Rosetta Stone is discovered.	**1799**
The Suez Canal is completed.	**1869**
British troops occupy Egypt.	**1882**
Britain declares Egypt a protectorate.	**1914**
Britain grants Egypt independence.	**1922**
The Muslim Brotherhood is founded.	**1928**
Army officers under Gamal Abdel Nasser overthrow King Farouk.	**1952**
Egypt is declared a republic.	**1953**
Gamal Abdel Nasser is elected president; he takes control of the Suez Canal.	**1956**
Israel occupies the Sinai in the Six-Day War.	**1967**
The Aswan High Dam begins operation.	**1970**
President Anwar el-Sadat and Israel's Menachem Begin sign the Camp David Accords.	**1978**
Anwar el-Sadat is assassinated; Hosni Mubarak becomes president.	**1981**
Dozens of tourists are killed near Luxor, allegedly by an Islamic group.	**1997**
A constitutional amendment allows for Egypt's first multiparty elections.	**2005**
The Egyptian revolution occurs; Hosni Mubarak resigns.	**2011**

World History

1776	The U.S. Declaration of Independence is signed.
1789	The French Revolution begins.
1865	The American Civil War ends.
1879	The first practical lightbulb is invented.
1914	World War I begins.
1917	The Bolshevik Revolution brings communism to Russia.
1929	A worldwide economic depression begins.
1939	World War II begins.
1945	World War II ends.
1957	The Vietnam War begins.
1969	Humans land on the Moon.
1975	The Vietnam War ends.
1989	The Berlin Wall is torn down as communism crumbles in Eastern Europe.
1991	The Soviet Union breaks into separate states.
2001	Terrorists attack the World Trade Center in New York City and the Pentagon near Washington, D.C.
2004	A tsunami in the Indian Ocean destroys coastlines in Africa, India, and Southeast Asia.
2008	The United States elects its first African American president.

Fast Facts

Official name: Arab Republic of Egypt

Capital: Cairo

Official language: Arabic

Cairo

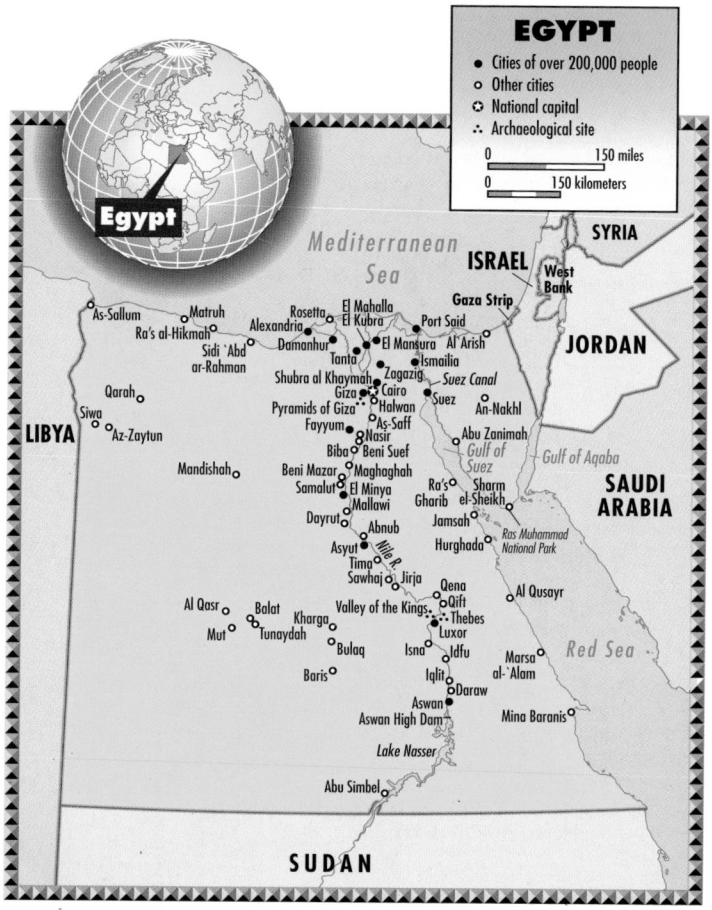

Egyptian flag

Official religion: Islam

Year of founding: As an independent nation, 1922; as a republic, 1953

National anthem: "*Biladi, Biladi, Biladi*" ("My Homeland, My Homeland, My Homeland")

Government: Republic

Chief of state: President

Head of government: Prime minister

Area: 386,660 square miles (1,001,450 sq km)

Latitude and longitude of geographic center: Approximately 27° N, 30° E

Bordering regions: Mediterranean Sea to the north; Gaza Strip, Israel, and the Red Sea to the east; Sudan to the south; and Libya to the west

Highest elevation: Jabal Katrina (Mount Catherine), 8,668 feet (2,642 m) above sea level

Lowest elevation: Qattara Depression, 435 feet (133 m) below sea level

Average temperatures: Alexandria: 58.5°F (14.7°C) in January, 79.3°F (26.3°C) in July; Aswan: 61.9°F (16.6°C) in January, 93°F (33.9°C) in July

Driest city: Aswan, 0.02 inches (0.05 cm) average annual precipitation

Wettest city: Alexandria, 7.9 inches (20 cm) average annual precipitation

Siwa Oasis

Great Pyramids

National population (2011 est.): 82,000,000

Population of major cities (2006 est.):

Cairo	6,758,581
Alexandria	4,110,015
Giza	2,681,863
Shubra al Khaymah	1,016,722
Halwan	643,327

Famous landmarks:

- ***Aswan High Dam and Lake Nasser,*** Aswan
- ***Egyptian Museum,*** Cairo
- ***Great Pyramids and Sphinx,*** Giza
- ***Step Pyramid of Djoser,*** Saqqara
- ***Temple of Amon,*** Karnak

Economy: Services make up the largest sector of Egypt's economy, with tourism as the major service industry. Egypt's leading manufactured goods are food products, petroleum products, metal products, and cotton textiles, a leading export. Petroleum and natural gas are Egypt's richest mineral resources, and petroleum is the major export. Cotton is the major crop, and others include sugarcane, wheat, rice, maize (corn), tomatoes, potatoes, and oranges.

Currency

Currency: The Egyptian pound (£E). In 2011, £E 5.97 was equal to US$1, and £E 1 was equal to US$0.17.

System of weights and measures: Metric system

Literacy rate (2006): 66%

College student

Naguib Mahfouz

Common Arabic words and phrases:

aywa	yes
la	no
assalaamu aleikum	hello
ma'a salaama	good-bye
minfadlik	please (to a woman)
minfadlak	please (to a man)
shukran	thank you
Feyn . . . ?	Where is . . . ?
Bekaam?	How much?

Prominent Egyptians:

Boutros Boutros-Ghali (1922–)
Secretary-general of the United Nations

Mohamed ElBaradei (1942–)
International Atomic Energy Agency director, Nobel Peace Prize winner

Hatshepsut (1500s–1400s BCE)
Female pharaoh

Naguib Mahfouz (1911–2006)
Nobel Prize–winning novelist

Menes (flourished ca. 3100 BCE)
Unifier of Upper and Lower Egypt

Muhammad Ali (1769–1849)
The father of modern Egypt

Gamal Abdel Nasser (1918–1970)
President

To Find Out More

Books

- Berg, Elizabeth. *Egypt*. New York: Marshall Cavendish Benchmark, 2010.
- Dell, Pamela. *Hatshepsut: Egypt's First Female Pharaoh*. Minneapolis: Compass Point Books, 2008.
- Heinrichs, Ann. *The Nile*. New York: Marshall Cavendish Benchmark, 2008.
- Katan, Norma Jean, and Barbara Mintz. *Hieroglyphs: The Writing of Ancient Egypt*. New York: Margaret K. McElderry, 2011.
- MacDonald, Fiona. *The Ancient Egyptians: Dress, Eat, Write and Play Just Like the Egyptians*. New York: Crabtree, 2008.
- Moscovitch, Arlene. *Egypt: the People*. New York: Crabtree, 2008.
- Perl, Lila. *Mummies, Tombs, and Treasure: Secrets of Ancient Egypt*. New York: Clarion Books, 2008.
- Sheen, Barbara. *Foods of Egypt*. Detroit: KidHaven Press, 2010.

DVDs

- *Ancient Lives*. Athena, 2009.
- *Ancient Technology in Egypt*. Adventures Unlimited Media, 2011.
- *Egypt: Pyramids and Mummies (History Classics)*. A&E Home Video, 2010.
- *Families of Egypt*. Master Communications Inc., 2006.
- *Mystery of the Nile*. Image Entertainment, 2008.

Web Sites

- **BBC History—Egyptians**
  www.bbc.co.uk/history
  /ancient/egyptians/
  To explore the world of ancient Egypt, from its pharaohs to its ordinary working people.

- **Children's University of Manchester—Ancient Egypt**
  www.childrensuniversity .manchester.ac.uk/interactives
  /history/egypt/egyptiangod.asp
  This interactive Web site teaches about Egyptian hieroglyphics, religion, pyramids, mummies, the number system, and more.

- **IndyKids!—Kids Take Part in Egypt's Revolution**
  http://indykids.net/main/2011/03
  /kids-take-part-in-egypts
  -revolution/
  See the 2011 Egyptian revolution through the eyes of kids who took part in it.

Embassies and Organizations

- **Egyptian Cultural and Educational Bureau**
  1303 New Hampshire Avenue NW
  Washington, DC 20036
  202/296-3888
  www.eecous.net

- **Embassy of Egypt**
  3521 International Court NW
  Washington, DC 20008
  202/895-5400
  www.egyptembassy.net

- **Embassy of Egypt in Canada**
  454 Laurier Avenue
  Ottawa, Ontario K1N 6R3
  Canada
  613/234-4931

- **Visit this Scholastic Web site for more information on Egypt:**
  www.factsfornow.scholastic.com

Index

Page numbers in *italics* indicate illustrations.

A

Abbasid caliphs, 52
Abu Simbel temple, 22
administrative courts, 69
Africa Cup of Nations soccer tournament, 114, *114*, 115
agriculture
  ancient Egypt, 37, 38, *38*
  Aswan High Dam and, 23, 82
  climate and, 81, 82
  crops, *74*, 81, *81*, 82, 109
  economy and, 78, 80
  employment in, 80
  fellahin, 91, 124
  flooding and, 23, 39
  irrigation, *14*, 23, 35, 55, 75, 82
  livestock, *81*, 89, 90, 118, 124, 125, 127
  Nile Delta, 19, *19*, 21, 34–35, 81
  trade and, 39
  villages, 91, 124
Ahmad Hamdi Tunnel, 82–83
airports, 85, *85*
Al-Azhar University, 53, 97
Alexander the Great, 21, 47–48, *47*
Alexandria, 18, 19, 21, *21*, 48, 49, 51, 52, *52*, 69, 82, 83, 85, 89, 91, 115, 120, 126, *126*, *127*
Ali, Muhammad, 56, 70
Al Jazeera news network, 87
Amon-Re (god), 41, *41*
Amr ibn al-As, 51
ancient Egypt
  afterlife, 42, 45, 104
  agriculture, 37, 38, *38*
  Alexander the Great, 21, 47–48, *47*
  Amon-Re (god), 41, *41*
  Anubis (god), 42
  Cleopatra (pharaoh), 48, 49, *49*
  common class, 38
  Djoser (pharaoh), 43
  dynasties, 37
  government, 38
  Hatshepsut (pharaoh), 45
  hieroglyphs, 34, 40, *40*, 56, *56*, 95
  Khafre (pharaoh), 43
  Khufu (pharaoh), 43
  map, *42*
  Menes (pharaoh), 37
  Menkaure (pharaoh), 43
  middle class, 38
  Middle Kingdom, *42*, 44
  New Kingdom, *42*, 44, 45–47
  Old Kingdom, *42*, 44
  oracles, 47
  Osiris (god), 42
  people, 37–38, 42
  pharaohs, *36*, 37–38, 39, 41, 42–43, 44, 45, *45*, 46, 47, 48, *48*, 49, 52, 70, 79, 93, 112
  Ptolemaic period, 48
  pyramids, 21, *21*, 28, 42–44, *43*, 70, 77
  Ramses II (pharaoh), 46, 70
  Ramses III (pharaoh), 46
  religion, 32, 41–42, *41*, 47
  scribes, 38
  Thoth (god), 32
  Thutmose III (pharaoh), 45
  tombs, 12, 42–43, 45, 46, *46*, 112
  Tutankhamen (pharaoh), *36*, 45, 45, 112
  upper class, 37–38
  women, 38
animal life
  Aswan High Dam and, 28
  birds, 32–33, *32*, *33*
  camels, 24, 25, *25*, 31–32, *31*, 86, 89
  caracals, *30*, 31
  climate and, 27
  fennecs, *26*, 29
  horses, 114–115
  hyenas, 28, *28*
  ibexes, 29
  livestock, *81*, 89, 90, 118, 124, 125, 127
  Nile River valley, 27
  pyramids and, 28
  religion and, 32
  rock hyraxes, 29
  rodents, 33
  scorpions, 29, *29*
  temples and, 28
  urban areas, 33
  wildcats, 30–31, *30*
Antony, Mark, 48–49, *49*
Anubis (god), 42
al-Aqqad, Abbas, 112
Arab Gas Pipeline, 79
Arabian Desert. *See* Eastern Desert.
Arabic language, 52, 56, 77, 82, 87, 94, *94*, 95, 99
Arabs, 51–52, 57, 59, 64, 91
Arab Spring movement, 8, 9–12, *12*, 61, 75, 85–86, 86, 90–91, 112
archaeology, 21, 55
artifacts, 39, 55, 112
arts, 39, *39*, 53, 94
Aswan, 18, 22, 43, 77, 82, 83, *87*, 93, *93*
Aswan High Dam, 22–23, *23*, 28, 58, 82, 93
Ayyubid dynasty, 53

B

Bahariya Oasis, 20, *100*
Barakat, Mohamed, *114*

Baris Oasis, 20
Battle of El Alamein, 57
Battle of the Pyramids, 55
Baybars (sultan), 54
Bedouins, 24, 31, 89, 91, 92, *92*
Begin, Menachem, 60
belly dancing, 112, 125
Ben Ezra Synagogue, 107, *107*
beverages, 118
Bibliotheca Alexandrina, 21
"Biladi, Biladi, Biladi" (national anthem), 66
birds, 32–33, *32*, *33*
Blue Nile River, 18, 19
Boutros-Ghali, Boutros, 71, *71*
Byzantine Empire, 50

C

Caesar, Julius, 48
cafés, 127, *127*
Cairo, 9, 11, 12, *12*, *13*, 19, 21, 43, 44, 51, 52, 53, 54, 55, 61, 69, 70, *70*, 71, *74*, 82, 83, 83, 85, 87, 88, 89, 90, 91, 97, 98, 101, 103, 106, 107, *107*, 109, 111, *111*, 112, *112*, 114, 115, *116*, 120, 121, *121*, 122, 125–126
Cairo International Airport, 85, *85*
Cairo Metro, 83, *83*
Cairo Opera House, 111, *111*
Cairo Trilogy (Naguib Mahfouz), 113
Cairo University, 97, *97*
caliphs (Muslim leaders), 52, 54, 55
camels, 24, 25, *25*, 31–32, *31*, 86, 89
Camp David Accords, 60
caracals, *30*, 31
cattle egrets, 33
cell phones, 86
ceramics, 39, *39*, 54
Champollion, Jean-François, 56
children, *13*, 96–97, 96, *102*, 125
Children of Gebelawi (Naguib Mahfouz), 113
Christianity, 11, 50, *51*, 53, 69, 71, 93, *95*, 103–107, *104*, *105*, *106*
Citadel of Saladin, 70, 101
cities. *See also* towns; villages.
  Alexandria, 18, 19, 21, *21*, 48, 49, 51, 52, *52*, 69, 82, 83, 85, 89, 91, 115, 120, 126, *126*, *127*
  Aswan, 18, *22*, 43, 77, 82, 83, *87*, 93, *93*
Cairo, 9, 11, 12, *12*, *13*, 19, 21, 43, 44, 51, 52, 53, 54, 55, 61, 69, 70, *70*, 71, *74*, 82, 83, 83, 85, 87, 88, 89, 90, 91, 97, 98, 101, 103, 106, 107, *107*, 109, 111, *111*, 112, *112*, 114, 115, *116*, 120, 121, *121*, 122, 125–126
  al-Fustat, 51
  Giza, 21, *21*, 43–44, 89, 91
  Halwan, 91
  Hurghada, 17, 85, *104*, 115
  Khan al-Khalili, 70, *108*, 109
  Luxor, 41, 61, 85
  Memphis, 43, 44
  Port Said, 89, 91
  Shubra al Khaymah, 21, 91
  Suez, *84*, 91
  Thebes, 44, 45, 46
City of the Dead, 122–123, *122*
Cleopatra (pharaoh), 48, 49, *49*
Cleopatra's Needles, 21
climate, 18, 19, 24–25, 81
clothing, 96, 99, 118–120, *119*, *120*
coastline, 19, 23, 24, 33, 35, 75, 82, 89, *126*
Colored Canyon, 24
communications, 85–87, 86, *87*
Constantine, emperor of Rome, 50
constitution, 59, *62*, 63, 65, 68, 69, 99
Coptic Church, 50, *51*, 71, 92, 93, 95–96, *95*, 100, 103–107, *104*, *105*, *106*
Coptic language, 52, 95–96
coral reefs, 17, *17*, 24, 33–34, *34*, 115
cotton, 81, 82, 109
court of cassation, 69
courts of general jurisdiction, 69
crafts, 39, *39*, 54, 109
crocodiles, 27–28
Crusades, 53
currency (Egyptian pounds), 77, *77*

D

Dahab, 115
Dakhla Oasis, 20
dancing, 112, 125
Darwish, Sayed, 66, 110
demotic script, 95
deserts, 15, 16–17, 25, *25*, *26*, *28*, *29*, *30*, *31*, *35*, *75*, *79*, *81*, *82*, *86*, *89*, *92*, *104*, *106*
Diab, Amr, 111
Diocletian, emperor of Rome, 50
Djoser (pharaoh), 43

E

Eastern Desert, 16, 79, 92
economy
  agriculture and, 78, 80
  currency (Egyptian pounds), 77, *77*
  debt, 57
  employment, 80
  exports, 78, 79
  government and, 91
  manufacturing, 21, 78–79, *78*, 80
  mining, 78, 79–80
  natural gas industry, 79–80
  oil industry, 79–80
  privatization, 61, 75
  services industry, 77
  Suez Canal and, 57
  textile industry, 78, *78*
  tourism, 77–78
  trade, 52–53, 84
  unemployment, 13, 75, 76
education, 21, 48, 53, 56, 71, 76, *76*, 93, 96–97, 96, 97, 99
Egyptian Museum, 70, 112, *112*
Egyptian Pharaohs soccer team, 114, *114*, 115
Egyptian pounds (currency), 77, *77*
Egyptian Radio and Television Union (ERTU), 87

ElBaradei, Mohamed, 73, *73*
electricity, 23, 123
English language, 77, 82, 87, 94
eucalyptus trees, 35
executive branch of government, 63, 65, 66–67

F

Farafra Oasis, 20
Farouk (king), 58, *58*, 59
Fatimid dynasty, 52, 53, 70
Fayyum settlement, 22, 35
fellahin (Nile villagers), 91, 123, 124
feluccas (flat-bottomed boats), 115
fennecs, 26, 29
film industry, 113, *113*
Five Pillars of Faith, 100
flamingos, 33
flooding, 19, *19*, 23, 39, 41, 82
foods, 39, 78, 81, 90, 99, 101–102, 104–105, *116*, 117–118, *118*, 124, 125
forests, 35
Freedom and Justice Party, 73
French language, 87, 94
ful (national dish), 118, *118*
al-Fustat, 51

G

geography
  coastline, 19, 23, 24, 33, 35, 75, 82, 89, *126*
  Colored Canyon, 24
  deserts, 15, 16–17, 25, 25, 26, 28, 29, 30, 31, 35, 75, 79, 81, 82, 86, 89, 92, 104, 106
  elevation, 15, 17, 18, 24
  islands, 70
  lakes, 18, 22, *22*
  land area, 15
  Lower Egypt, 15
  mountains, 18, 24, 25
  Nile River, 15, 18–19
  oases, 20, 22
  Qattara Depression, 17, 18
  Sinai Peninsula, 15–16, 24
  Suez Canal, 16, *16*
  Upper Egypt, 15
  wadis (ravines), 17
Gezira Island, 70, 111
al-Ghad Party, 73
Ghonim, Wael, 85–86
Giza, 21, *21*, 43–44, 89, 91
government
  administrative courts, 69
  ancient Egypt, 38
  censorship, 9, 86–87, 113
  constitution, 59, *62*, 63, 65, 68, 69, 99
  court of cassation, 69
  courts of general jurisdiction, 69
  economy and, 61, 75, 79, 91
  elections, 61, *62*, 64–65, 68, 73
  executive branch, 63, 65, 66–67
  Freedom and Justice Party, 73
  independence, 57, 58
  judicial branch, 63, 65, 69
  laws, 13, 58, 63, 67, *67*, 68, 69, 71, 96
  legislative branch, 63, 64–65, 67–68, *67*, 68, 71, 72
  military, 58, 60, 61, 63, 68
  Mugama'a (government building), 70
  muhafazat (governorates), 69, 71
  Muslim Brotherhood (MB), 71–73, *72*
  Napoléon and, 55
  National Democratic Party (NDP), 64
  newspapers and, 87
  People's Assembly, 63, 64, 67–68, *67*, 71, 72
  political parties, 71–73, *72*
  presidents, 9, *11*, 22, 58, 59–60, *59*, 60, 63, 64, 66–67
  prime ministers, 58
  privatization, 61, 75, 79
  religion and, 69, 71, 99, 107
  Shura Council, 63, 68, *68*
  Supreme Constitutional Court, 69
  treaties, 60
  vice presidents, 63
  women and, 67, 68
Great Britain, 55, 57, 58, 87
Great Pyramid, 43, *43*
Great Sphinx, 21, 44, *44*, 77
Great Temple of Ramses II, *22*, 46, 77
Greco-Roman Museum, 21
Greek Empire, 47, 48, *50*
Greek Orthodox Church, 24, 107
Gulf of Aqaba, 24, 59
Gulf of Suez, 24

H

hajj (pilgrimage), 100, 123
Halwan, 91
Hamed, Marwan, 113
Harrania, 109
Hassan (sultan), 70
Hatshepsut (pharaoh), 45, 133
health care, 22, 71
Herodotus (Greek historian), 13
herons, 32
hieroglyphs, 34, 40, *40*, 56, *56*, 95
historical maps. *See also* maps.
  Ancient Egypt, *42*
  Greek and Roman Egypt, *50*
  Napoléon's Invasion of Egypt, 55
holidays
  national, 120, 121, *121*
  religious, 101–103, *102*, 103, 104–105, 106–107
Holy Family, 105
horsemanship, 114–115
housing, 90, 93, 120–123, *121*, *123*
Hurghada, 17, 85, *104*, 115
Hussein, Taha, 112
hydroelectricity, 23
hyenas, 28, *28*

I

ibexes, 29

ibises, 32, *32*
'Id al-Adha holiday, 103, *103*
'Id al-Fitr holiday, 102
iftar (Ramadan feast), 101–102
Imhotep (architect), 43
insect life, 33
International Atomic Energy Agency (IAEA), 73
Internet, 85–86, 86, 86–87
irrigation, *14*, 23, 35, 55, 75, 82, 89
Islamic religion. *See also* religion.
  calendar, 101
  caliphs (leaders), 52, 54, 55
  clothing and, 118, 119
  conversion, 104
  fasting, 100, 101, 102
  Five Pillars of Faith, 100
  followers of, 11, 100
  fundamentalists, 60, 61, 71, 113
  government and, 69, 71
  hajj (pilgrimage), 100, 123
  holidays, 101–103, *102, 103*
  holy day, 126
  'Id al-Adha holiday, 103, *103*
  'Id al-Fitr holiday, 102
  law of, 69, 118, 119
  Mecca, Saudi Arabia and, 100, 101, *101*, 123
  mosques, 70, 98, 100, *100*
  moulids (festivals), 103
  Muhammad (prophet), 51, 52, 101, 103
  patron saints, 103
  prayer, 100, *103*
  Qur'an (holy book), 99, 101
  Ramadan (holy month), 100, 101–102, *102*
  Ras al-Sana al-Hegira (Islamic New Year), 103
  Shi'i Muslims, 99
  Sultan Hassan Mosque, 98
  Sunni Muslims, 99
Israel, 57, 59–60, 61, 92

J

Jabal Katrina (Mount Catherine), 18, 24
Jawhar (Fatimid general), 52
al-Jihad fundamentalist group, 60
Judaism, 69, 107, *107*
judicial branch of government, 63, 65, 69

K

Karnak temples, 41, *41*, 44, 46, 77
Khafre (pharaoh), 43
khamsin (wind), 25
Khan al-Khalili, 70, *108*, 109
Khan, Mohamed, 113, *113*
Kharga Oasis, 18, 20
Khufu (pharaoh), 43
Kulthum, Umm, 110–111

L

Lake Nasser, 18, 22, *22*, 33, 82, 93
languages, 34, 40, *40*, 52, 56, 56, 77, 82, 87, 94, *94*, 95–96, 99, 107
legislative branch of government, 63, 64–65, 67–68, *67*, 68
Library of Alexandria, 21
literature, 53, 112–113, 113
livestock, *81*, 89, 90, 118, 124, 125, 127
local governments, 69, 71
lotus flowers, 35, *35*
Lower Egypt, 15, 34, 37
Luxor, 41, 61, 85

M

Mahfouz, Asmaa, 86
Mahfouz, Naguib, 112, 113, *113*
Mamelukes (Ayyubid soldiers), 53–54, *54*, 55, 70, 114–115
mancala (board game), 124, *124*
mangrove forests, 35
manufacturing, 21, 78–79, *78*, 80
maps. *See also* historical maps.
  Cairo, *70*
  geopolitical, *10*
  population density, *90*
  resources, *79*
  topographical, *18*
marine life, *17*, 33–34, *34*, 115
mastabas (tombs), 42–43
Mecca, Saudi Arabia, 100, 101, *101*, 123
Memphis, 43, 44
Menes (pharaoh), 37
Menkaure (pharaoh), 43
Middle Kingdom, 44
mining, 78, 79–80
Montgomery, Bernard, 57
mosques, 70, 98, 100, *100*
moulids (festivals), 103
Mount Catherine. *See* Jabal Katrina.
Mount Sinai, 24
Mubarak, Hosni, 9, *11*, 60–61, 65, 73, 86
Mugama'a (government building), 70
muhafazat (governorates), 69, 71
Muhammad (prophet), 51, 52, 99, 101, 103
al-Mu'izz (caliph), 52
museums, 21, *45*, 48, 56, 70, 111, 112, *112*
music, 37–38, 66, 110–111, *110*, *111*, 125
Muslim Brotherhood (MB), 71–73, *72*
Muslims. *See* Islamic religion.

N

Nabataean culture, 94
Nagy, Mohamed "Gedo," 115, *115*
Nakhl, 18
Napoléon, emperor of France, 55, *55*
Nasif, Malak Hifni, 113
Nasser, Gamal Abdel, 22, 58, 59, *59*
national anthem, 66, 110
National Democratic Party (NDP), 64–65, 71, 73
national flag, 64, *64*
national flower, 35, *35*
national holidays, 120, 121, *121*
National Progressive Unionist Party, 73

national soccer team, 114, *114*
natural gas industry, 79–80
necropolises, 46
New Kingdom, 44, 45–47
newspapers, 87, *87*
New Valley oases, 20
New Wafd Party, 73
Nile International Rowing Competition, 115
Nile River, *14*, 15, 18–19, *19*, 20, 21, 22, 23, *23*, 27, 32, 33, 35, 39, 43, 70, 77, 80, 82, 89, *91*, 124
Nile River Delta, 19, 21, 23, 30, 34, 35, 37, 79, 81, 82, 89
Nobel Prize, 60, 73, 112
nomads, 31, 89, 92, *92*
Nubians, 93, *93*

O

oases, 20, *20*, 22, 82, 89
Octavian, emperor of Rome, 48–49, *49*
October War, 60
oil industry, 17, 79–80
Old Kingdom, 44
Osiris (god), 42
Ottoman Empire, 54–55, 56
oud (musical instrument), 110, *110*

P

papyrus plants, 34–35
Pasha, Ismail, 57
Pasha, Muhammad Ali, 21
Pasha, Said, 56
Patriarch of Alexandria, 106, *106*
people
  ancient Egypt, 37–38, 42
  Arabs, 51–52, 57, 59, 91
  Bedouins, 24, 31, 89, 91, 92, *92*
  children, *13*, 96–97, *96*, *102*, *116*, 125, *126*
  clothing, 96, 99, 118–120, *119*, *120*
  communications, 85–87, 86, 87
  Copts, 93, 95–96, 95
  education, 21, 48, 53, 56, 71, 76, *76*, 93, 96–97, *96*, *97*, 99
  elections, 62, 63
  employment, 75, 77, 89, 90, 97
  families, 97, *102*, *103*
  fellahin, 91, 123, 124
  foods, 39, 78, 81, 99, 101–102, 104–105, *116*, 117–118, *118*, 124, 125
  health care, 22, 71
  housing, 90, 93, 120–123, *121*, *123*
  languages, 34, 40, *40*, 52, 56, *56*, 77, 82, 87, 94, *94*, 95–96, 99, 107
  life expectancy, 42, 90
  literacy rate, 97
  marriage, 67, 112, 125, *125*
  Nabataeans, 94
  nomads, 24, 31, 89, 92, *92*
  Nubians, 93, *93*
  population, 19, 21, 70, 88, 89, 90, 90, 91, 122
  poverty, 13, *13*, 90, 93
  rural areas, 123, *123*, 124
  Shi'i Muslims, 99
  Sunni Muslims, 99
  unemployment, 13, 75, 76, 90–91, 125
  urban areas, 89, 125–127
  weddings, 112, 125, *125*
  women, 38, 68, 93, 97, *97*, 113, 118–119, *119*
  youth bubble, 90–91
People's Assembly, 63, 64–65, 67–68, *67*, 71, 72
Persian Achaemenian Empire, 47
pharaohs, *36*, 37–38, 39, 41, 42–43, 44, 45, *45*, 46, 47, 48, *48*, 49, 52, 70, 79, 93, 112
Pharaonic Village, 21
Pharos Lighthouse, 21, 52
Philae temple, 22, 77
pied kingfishers, 32
plant life
  eucalyptus trees, 35
  lotus flowers, 35, *35*
  mangrove forests, 35
  oases, *20*
  palm trees, 20, *20*, 35
  papyrus, 34–35
  tamarisk shrubs, 35
  water hyacinths, 35
pollution, 17, 125
Pompey's Pillar, 21
population, 19, 21, 70, 88, 89, 90, 90, 91, 122
Port Said, 89, 91
poverty, 13, *13*, 90, 93
precipitation, 18, 19, 25
Ptolemaic period, 48, 95
pyramids, 21, *21*, 28, 42–44, *43*, 70, 77

Q

Qadi, Younis-al, 66
Qattara Depression, 17, 18
Qur'an (holy book), 99, 101

R

radio, 87
railways, 70, 83, *83*
rainfall. *See* precipitation.
Ramadan (holy month), 100, 101–102, *102*
Ramses II (pharaoh), 46, 70, 77
Ramses III (pharaoh), 46
Ramses Wissa Wassef Art Centre, 109
Ras al-Sana al-Hegira (Islamic New Year), 103
Ras Muhammad National Park, 115
Red Sea, 17, *17*, 24, 33, *34*, 35, 77, 115
religion. *See also* Islamic religion.
  afterlife, 42, 45, 104
  ancient Egypt, 32, 41–42, *41*, 47
  animal life and, 32
  baptisms, 105, *105*
  Ben Ezra Synagogue, 107, *107*

Christianity, 11, 50, *51*, 53, 69, 71, 93, 95, 103–107, *104*, *105*, *106*
conversion, 104
Coptic Church, 50, *51*, 71, 92, 93, 95–96, 95, 100, 103–107, *104*, *105*, *106*
Crusades, 53
fasting, 104–105
government and, 69, 71, 99, 107
holidays, 101–103, *102*, 103, 104–105, 106–107
Holy Family, 105
Judaism, 69, 107, *107*
Patriarch of Alexandria, 106, *106*
Saint Catherine's Greek Orthodox monastery, 24
reptilian life, 27–28, 29
roadways, 82, 125, 127
rock hyraxes, 29
Roda Island, 70
Roman Empire, 48, 50, *50*
Rommel, Erwin, 57
Rosetta Stone, 56, *56*

S

el-Sadat, Anwar, 59–60, *60*
Safaga, 85, 115
Sahara Desert, 16
Saint Catherine's Greek Orthodox monastery, 24
Saladin (warrior), 53, *53*, 70, 101
Saqqara, 43
satellites, 87
scorpions, 29, *29*
scribes, 38
scuba diving, 115
Selim (sultan), 54
service industry, 77
Sham an-Nessim holiday, 121, *121*
Sharm el-Sheikh, 24, 85, 115, 126
Shi'i Muslims, 99
Shubra al Khaymah, 21, 91
Shura Council, 63, 68, *68*
Sinai Peninsula, 15–16, 24, 82, 89, 92, *104*, 115
Siwa Oasis, 20, *20*, 47
Six-Day War, 59
soccer, 114, *114*, 115, *115*
Sphinx. *See* Great Sphinx.
sports, 114–115, *114*, *115*
Star of the East Museum, 111
Step Pyramid, 43
Suez, *84*, 91
Suez Canal, 16, *16*, 55, 56–57, 59, 60, 82, 84–85, *84*, 89
Sultan Hassan Mosque, 98
Sunni Muslims, 99
Supreme Constitutional Court, 69

T

Tahrir Square, 9, 11, 12, 61, 85
tamarisk shrubs, 35
Taymur, Mahmud, 112–113
television, 87
temperatures, 18, *25*
Temple of Amon (Karnak), 41, *41*, 44, 46, 77
terrorism, 60, 61, 78, 113
textile industry, 78, *78*
Thebes, 44, 45, 46
Theodosius, emperor of Rome, 50
Thoth (god), 32
Thutmose III (pharaoh), 45
tombs, 45, 46, *46*, 112, 122, *122*
tourism, 21, 24, 35, 77–78
towns. *See also* cities; villages.
coastal towns, 17, 24
Dahab, 115
governments, 71
patron saints, 103
Rosetta, 56
Safaga, 85, 115
Sharm el-Sheikh, 24, 85, 115, 126
tourism, 24
trade, 52–53, 84
transportation, *16*, 23, 24, 25, *25*, 43, 52–53, 56–57, 59, 75, 82–83, *83*, 84–85, 84, 125, 127
Turkish Ottoman Empire, 54
Tutankhamen (pharaoh), *36*, 45, *45*, 77, 112

U

Umayyad caliphs, 52
United Nations, 57, 71
United States, 15, 58, 60, 61, 79, 87
University of Cairo, 21
Upper Egypt, 15, 25, 35, 37

V

Valley of the Kings, 46, *46*, 77
Valley of the Queens, 46
villages. *See also* cities; towns.
fellahin, 91, 123, 124
foods, 117–118, 124
government, 71
Harrania, 109
Pharaonic Village, 21
tourism, 77

W

Wadi Natrun, 106
wadis (ravines), 17
water, *14*, 22–23, *22*, *23*, 35, 55, 75, 81, 82
water hyacinths, 35
water sports, 115
Western Desert, 16–17, 20, 75, 79, 82, 92
White Nile River, 18
wildcats, 30–31, *30*
wildlife. *See* animal life; insect life; marine life; plant life; reptilian life.
women, 38, 68, *93*, 97, *97*, 113, 118–119, *119*
World War I, 57
World War II, 57

Meet the Author

ANN HEINRICHS FELL IN LOVE WITH FARAWAY places as a child while reading Doctor Dolittle books and *Peter Freuchen's Book of the Seven Seas*. Now she tries to cover as much of the world as possible. She has traveled through most of the United States and much of Europe, as well as Africa, the Middle East, and East Asia.

Heinrichs's travels in Egypt gave her rich insights into the country's culture, history, and natural resources. She rode camels, trekked through deserts, scaled massive rock formations, climbed Mount Sinai, shopped in bazaars, and visited the pyramids and the Sphinx. An Egyptian carpet weaver even showed her how to work his weaving loom. Riding a camel was one of her favorite experiences. "Camels are much more comfortable than horses," she insists. "They move along with a gentle lurch that's almost hypnotizing."

Heinrichs grew up roaming the woods of Arkansas. Now she lives in Chicago, Illinois. She is the author of more than two hundred books for children and young adults on American, European, Asian, and African history and culture.

"When I'm starting a country book," Heinrichs says, "I head for the library's reference department. Some of my favorite resources are United Nations publications, *Europa World Year Book*, and the periodicals databases. "For this book, I also read English-language issues of *Al-Ahram* and tuned in to Al Jazeera to get a feel for Egyptians' current interests and viewpoints. I have some Egyptian friends, too, so I interviewed them about the impacts of the revolution, as well as conditions in Egypt in general."

Heinrichs holds bachelor's and master's degrees in piano performance and, most recently, a master of library and information science (MLIS) degree. Her favorite library internship sites were at the Library of Congress, the Chicago Academy of Sciences, and Chicago's Newberry Library. For fun, she enjoys bicycling along Chicago's lakefront and kayaking.

Photo Credits

Photographs © 2012:

age fotostock: back cover (Image Asset Management Ltd.), 74 (José Fuste Raga), 84 (Sylvain Grandadam), 54 (The British Library), 112 (Toño Labra), 111 (Wael Hamdan);

Alamy Images: 26 (Amar and Isabelle Guillen - Guillen Photography), 85 (Andrew Holt), 7 bottom, 33 (Arco Images GmbH), 19 (Barry Iverson), 122 (Blaine Harrington III), 32 (blickwinkel/Schmidbauer), 96 (Boaz Rottem), 121 top (Brian Harris), 8, 97, 119, 133 top (Claudia Wiens), cover, 6 (David Ball), 116 (dbimages), 22 (F1 Online digitale Bildagentur GmbH), 29 (Ian M Butterfield (Egypt)), 123 (imagebroker), 52 (Interfoto), 110 (Jason Smalley/Wildscape), 20, 87, 131 bottom (John Frumm/Hemis), 45 (Larry Lilac), 125 (Luis Orteo/Hemis), 86 (Michael Honegger), 78 (Michael Ventura), 120 (Patrick Frilet/MARKA), 126 (Peter M. Wilson/Corbis Nomad), 93 (Reinhard Dirscherl), 92 (Travel Pictures/Pictures Colour Library), 76, 118 (travelpixs), 23 (Walter Bibikow/Jon Arnold Images Ltd.);

AP Images: 113 top, 133 bottom (Amr Nabil), 72 (Asmaa Waguih), 47 (North Wind Picture Archives), 11 (Pablo Martinez Monsivais), 106 (Peter Kollanyi/MTI), 12 (Sipa), 67, 68;

Bridgeman Art Library/Johann Heinrich Tischbein/Neue Galerie, Kassel, Germany/Museumslandschaft Hessen Kassel Ute Brunzel: 49;

Corbis Images: 95 (Dave Bartruff), 73 (David Degner/ZUMA Press), 71 (Eric Fougere/VIP Images), 98 (Julian Love/JAI), 60 (Kevin Fleming), 127 (Rob Howard), 40 (Sandro Vannini), 108, 130 left (Stuart Westmorland), 105 (Thomas Hartwell), 81 (Wolfgang Kaehler);

Getty Images: 2 (Adam Jones/The Image Bank), 113 bottom (Amro Maraghi/AFP), 88 (Cris Bouroncle/AFP), 31 (Ed Lallo/Photolibrary), 21 bottom (Hisham Ibrahim/PhotoDisc), 107 (Hisham Ibrahim/Photographer's Choice), 16 (Jacques Marais/Gallo Images), 21 top (Keren Su/The Image Bank), 13, 102, 121 bottom (Khaled Desouki/AFP), 101 (Mustafa Ozer/AFP), 83 (Peter Macdiarmid);

Media Bakery: 25, 30, 100;

Newscom: 41 (Herve Champollion/akg-images), 115 (imago sportfotodienst), 114 (Issouf Sanogo/AFP/Getty Images), 62 (Mahmud Hams/AFP/Getty Images), 103 (ZUMA Press);

Shutterstock, Inc.: 43, 132 top (Andresr), 77, 132 bottom (Daniel Wiedemann), 28 (Hector Conesa), 104 (Pecold), 44 (Pius Lee), 64, 131 top (Route66);

Superstock, Inc.: 34 (age fotostock), 7 top, 17 (Douglas Sprangler VWPics), 48 (Image Asset Management Ltd.), 35 (imagebroker.net), 14 (Peter Barritt), 91 (Robert Harding Picture Library), 46 (Stock Connection);

The Granger Collection: 36 (Rue des Archives), 38, 51, 53, 56;

The Image Works: 39 (Art Media/Heritage-Images), 124 (Fishman/ullstein bild), 58 (SZ Photo/Scherl), 59 (Tony Vaccaro/akg-images).

Maps by XNR Productions, Inc.